'I Visua in Social Theory

The scholar who ... does little else than handle
books ... ultimately forgets entirely and completely the capacity for thinking for himself ... all he
does is react. The scholar exhausts his whole
strength in saying either 'yes' or 'no' to matter that
has already been thought out .... With my own
eyes I have seen gifted, richly endowed and free-
spirited natures already 'read to ruins' at thirty.

                                        Friedrich Nietzsche

the time has come for sociology to renounce
worldly successes, so to speak, and take on the
esoteric character which befits all science. Thus it
will gain in dignity and authority what it will
perhaps lose in popularity. For so long as it remains
embroiled in partisan struggles and is content to
elaborate, with indeed more logic than is commonly employed, common ideas, and in consequence presumes no special competence, it has
no right to speak authoritatively enough to quell
passions and dispel prejudices. Assuredly the time is
still remote when it will be able effectively to play
this role. Yet from this very moment onwards, we
must work to place it in a position to fulfil this part.

                                        Emile Durkheim

The Visual
in Social Theory

ANTHONY WOODIWISS

THE ATHLONE PRESS
LONDON & NEW YORK

To my mother, with love

First published in 2001 by
THE ATHLONE PRESS
A Continuum imprint
The Tower Building, 11 York Road, London SE1 7NX
370 Lexington Avenue, New York, NY 10017-6503

© 2001 Anthony Woodiwiss

Anthony Woodiwiss has asserted his right under the Copyright, Designs and Patents
Act 1988, to be identified as the author of this work

British Library Cataloguing in Publication Data
*A catalogue record for this book is available
from the British Library.*

ISBN 0 485 00422 4 HB
0 485 00618 9 PB

Library of Congress Cataloging-in-Publication Data

Woodiwiss, Anthony.
The visual in social theory / Anthony Woodiwiss.
   p. cm.
Includes bibliographical references and index.
ISBN 0-485-00422-4 (case : alk. paper) — ISBN 0-485-00618-9 (pbk. : alk. paper)
1. Sociology. 2. Social perception. 3. Visual perception–Social aspects. I. Title.

HM585.W66 2001
301–dc21

00-046917

Typeset by Aarontype Limited, Easton, Bristol
Printed and bound in Great Britain by
MPG Books Ltd, Bodmin, Cornwall

Contents

List of Figures

Preface

This is a time of relative quiescence in social theory and among the various interested parties in Sociology and other disciplines. With the waning of postmodernism and for the first time in forty years, there is neither a dominant orthodoxy nor a radical insurgency threatening to overturn it. The wild movements of the theoretical pendulum that, beginning in the 1960s and, crudely put, saw a strong swing towards system countered by one towards action, followed by a swing back to structure which was in turn countered by one towards culture and deconstruction seem to have lost their momentum. The present calm therefore provides a long overdue opportunity for taking and, indeed, clearing stock. That said, any such activity implies the ending of the calm since it requires the application of a standard that enables one to distinguish what should be retained from what should be discarded.

Despite its title, this is not a book about the visual arts, media images or even social representations, except tangentally. Rather, it is about *how* social theories and theorists see, or think they see, the world. Nevertheless, the standard I have chosen to apply is one that has been widely influential in art criticism, namely that produced by the difference between 'vision' and 'visuality'. This is a distinction that has long been present in Western thought about sight but which owes its current prominence to the recent work of Martin Jay (1993) and collections edited by Hal Foster (1988) and David Levin

(1993). The point of the distinction is to register the difference between conceptualising sight as a supposedly natural faculty – vision – and conceptualising it as a historical and social construct – visuality. In other words and in one way at least, it is simply another way of making the familiar sociological distinction between that position that privileges observation – so-called naïve empiricism – and those who argue that observation is always either value or theory laden – virtually all other positions in social theory. Given this similarity, why do we need another way of making the distinction?

The long answer to this question is provided by this book as a whole, while the short answer is that sociological crime marches on. That is, the current threats to the sociological enterprise include not only a long-established, theoretically naïve empiricism but also a more recent empirically careless theoreticism. And while the latter escapes censure when the familiar standard is applied because it assumes the theory-dependence of vision, this is not the case when the vision/visuality variant of the distinction is applied. This is because the new way of making the distinction reaches both the familiar problem posed by empiricism and, to coin a phrase, parts of the sociological enterprise that are not reached by the older way. More specifically, it reaches the assumptions that theories carry as to how their component concepts see and therefore refer to the world.

Thus the vision/visuality distinction enables one to distinguish between and differentially evaluate two types of non-empiricist social theory. All varieties of non-empiricist social theory acknowledge that their concepts produce somewhat artificial representations of social reality rather than facsimiles of it. However, they may be distinguished and differentially evaluated on the basis of how they make their representations. On the one hand, there are those varieties of theory that apply their own frankly artificial visual templates to the world. They should be retained because the artifice manifest in their creation and application makes them contestable and corrigible. On the other, there are those that claim their templates to be simply pictures or mappings of what is. They should be cleared for at least three reasons. First, they radically over-simplify what is involved in sociological seeing. Second, the claim that they are pictures both makes empirical research unnecessary and renders any concepts so produced useless for explanatory purposes. Third, what is socially visible is not necessarily what is sociologically most important. Indeed, given the contemporary pervasiveness of what Andrew Wernick (1991) has termed 'promotional culture' – i.e. the subordination of information and even knowledge to selling and 'spinning' – it would seem wise to assume that things are not as they appear to be. In the absence of such scepticism the danger is that social theory becomes simply an aspect of promotional culture rather than its potential antidote. Hence the critical attention paid to such concepts as modernity, postmodernity and globalisation in this effort to restore some autonomy to the way in which social theory sees the world.

Despite its brevity, the stocktaking and clearance that follows covers a great deal of ground and was made possible by many conversations and arguments conducted over a long period of time. Among the many people whom I should thank, I can only remember the following: Alan Dawe, Paul Hirst, José López, Malcolm Ashmore, Ted Benton, Garry Potter, Sean Nixon, Paul Gilroy, Harold Wolpe, Rob Stones, Yao Jen-To,

Nicos Mouzelis, John Holmwood, Ian Craib, John Scott, Angela and Roger Woodiwiss, George Kolankiewicz, Aya Tokita, Gordon Marshall, Mike Featherstone, Bob Jessop, Paul Sutton, Mersut Ergun, Fehti Acikel, Bryan Turner and, inevitably, Kathianne Hingwan and Frank Pearce. I would also like to express my appreciation to several cohorts of MA 'Current Disputes' students at Essex during the late 1990s for their indulgence while I developed some of these ideas. Finally, I would like to acknowledge my debt to my colleagues on the board of *Economy and Society*, from whom I have learnt a great deal about the variety of theoretical discourse and the possibility of mutual learning. More particularly, I owe a special debt to Mike Gane (1988) for writing a whole book on Durkheim's *Rules* and so alerting me to its continuing fecundity as a source of sociological renewal.

Most of the manuscript was written between October 1998 and February 1999 while I was the fortunate recipient of a fellowship from the Department of Sociology of the Universidad Autonoma de Querétaro in Mexico. The conditions in the beautiful Casa Universitaria were perfect for writing and I wish to thank the staff of both the Department and the Casa, especially Augusto and Maria del Carmen Peon-Solis, Ana and Paco Diaz, Marta Gloria Morales, Teresa, Antonio and Teodora for making my visit both possible and highly enjoyable. Finally, I would also like to thank the Fuller Fund of the Department of Sociology at the University of Essex for financing my travel to Mexico and the Department of Sociology at City University for financing my return!

INTRODUCTION

Why Problematise the Visual?

Why vision and visuality, why these terms? Although vision suggests sight as a physical operation, and visuality sight as a social fact, the two are not opposed as nature to culture: vision is social and historical too, and visuality involves the body and the psyche. Yet neither are they identical: the difference between the terms signals a difference within the visual – between the mechanism of sight and its historical techniques, between the datum of vision and its discursive determinations – a difference, many differences, among how we see, how we are able, allowed or made to see, and how we see this seeing or the unseen therein. With its own rhetoric and representations, each scopic regime seeks to close out these differences: to make of its many social visualities one essential vision, or to order them in a natural hierarchy of sight. It is important then, to slip these superimpositions out of focus, to disturb the given array of visual facts (it may be the only way to see them at all)

(Foster, 1988, p. ix)

It would be very difficult to provide a better beginning to the present argument than that represented by Hal Foster's explication of the differences and relations between the concepts of

1

vision and visuality, and the critical possibilities thereby created. Consequently I will not try and will instead begin by outlining how what follows is structured by these differences, relations and critical possibilities. My starting point is therefore that the popular and intellectual privileging of vision in Western cultures is mistaken. As all varieties of non-empiricist social theory have recognised, at least until recently, to privilege vision over the other senses and the intellect (ocularcentrism) as both the chief provider of reliable sense data and the best mode of checking its accuracy is mistaken, since what we see is as much affected by the positions in time, space and social life from which we look – in this case, the visualities which we inhabit – as any other activity. Thus they have also recognised the need to guard against such privileging in their investigations. However, what they have been much less sensitive to, at least consciously, is the need to guard against any such privileging with respect to their concepts and theories or, in other words, the terms in which they envision the social and so both prepare it for investigation and summarise their results.

Thus I will be looking at the development and present state of social theory and judging its adequacy according to the degree to which it rests upon a recognition of the need to guard against ocularcentrism in the activity of theorising itself; that is, according to the degree to which its component concepts are regarded as products of a social system of picturing rather than individually created pictures of social life. However, since social theorists are wordsmiths rather than visual artists, I will be taking their assumptions as to the nature of language both as a proxy for and as an instantiation of their assumptions concerning the status they accord vision. This is because, like many others (Jay, 1993; Levin, 1993), it seems to me that improvements in our understanding of the nature of language have depended upon movements away from regarding words as a collection of pictures or representations of things and actions in the world and towards regarding them as part of a social apparatus for making things and actions visible or signifying them. That is, the move from regarding what is seen as a product of simple vision to seeing it as a product of a visuality or system of visualisation is the other side of the coin represented by the shift from regarding language as a collection of pictures to seeing it as a system of picturing.

The story I will tell on this basis has an ironic dimension since, while the classical theorists, namely Karl Marx, Max Weber and Emile Durkheim, contributed hugely to these conjoint shifts, some of their more recent progeny have failed to appreciate let alone build on their achievement. That is, while the classical theorists produced verbal representations of social life that, to use Foster's words, 'disturb[ed] the given array of visual facts', many of their successors have either simply repeated the given array, as has increasingly been the case in the work of Anthony Giddens, or magnified certain and, irony of ironies, specifically the visual aspects of it out of all proportion, as in the case of the Postmodernists. This, or so I will argue, is because they have lost the founders' intuition that it is visualities rather than vision that govern what we see (for another example of this loss, see John Urry's [2000, pp. 80–93] recent elision of vision and visuality). The consequence is that, in too many instances, contemporary Sociology's picture of the world could be superimposed over that produced by the governing Western common sense without any loss of focus — see the discussions of

3

the concept of modernity in Chapter 3, postmodernism in Chapter 4 and globalisation in the Conclusion. This is because, or so I will argue, some of its producers have unknowingly been suborned by visualities that are external to social science because they have failed to carry out fully their duty to be methodologically reflexive.

This, then, is why social theory currently requires the problematisation of the visual, namely to restore a degree of autonomy to its visuality and therefore restore its scientific and critical edge. This is also why the most obvious place to start looking for the necessary tools is the work of the classical theorists – at least in their own time they were able, again to quote Foster, to 'slip the superimpositions out of focus'. How exactly they did this will be explained in detail in Chapter 1. All that requires noting for now is that it was the fact that they worked up, so to speak, their theories in the context of substantive researches carried out for explanatory purposes that, in part at least, accounted for their success in disturbing the settled vision of the social. Thus another of my central arguments will be that any worthwhile reworking or extension of their concepts will likewise require their application in such a context if it is to be more than simply a restatement or, worse, a bowdlerisation.

At the heart of our current difficulties is a scandal so shocking that we hardly dare talk about it – the fact that we still have no at all robust conception of our defining object of interest – social structure – or, worse, do not realise that we have at least the beginnings of one. That is, we have no settled template of the social to superimpose over those of common sense or ideology. Hence the awkwardness and fast talking of all teachers of introductory sociology courses when they are asked to define this most taken-for-granted of terms within our discipline – after their first year, students learn that not asking this question is a price that has to be paid if they are to enter the sociological guild. José López (1999) has recently recounted with great clarity and considerable sympathy the travails of sociologists as they have wrestled with this problem. In order neither to steal his thunder nor excuse anyone the task of getting to grips with his argument, I will not even provide a brief summary here. Nevertheless, much of what I will have to say complements what he argues.

In sum, then, at the core of both my effort to diagnose the causes of our current intellectual seizure with respect to the concept of social structure and the recuperative regime that I will suggest is my belief that what has been missing from the sociological tradition is a fully self-conscious acknowledgement of the danger inherent in an overdependence on vision and therefore lack of appreciation of the full significance of language, not simply as a dimension of sociality but also, more impor-tantly within the present context, as our medium of theoretical expression. The postmodernists and the protagonists of Cultural Studies more broadly have taught us much that is of value on the first score but, for reasons that I will explain at length in Chap-ter 4, they have obscured just as much from us on the second.

SOCIOLOGISTS AND LANGUAGE:
THE NEGLECT OF SAUSSURE'S REVOLUTION

Sociologists may be divided into two camps in their con-scious attitudes towards language and therefore their conscious understandings of the visual status of their concepts. On the one hand, there is the positive, Neo-Kantian tradition exemplified by such as Max Weber and the phenomenologists, as well as the symbolic interactionists and ethnomethodologists. For this tradition, the fact that, contrary to Humean inductivism, sociological observers share the capacity for language with their human subject matter is the source of their great advantage over natural scientists in that, given the observance of certain relativising protocols, it enables them to see or understand the social in itself or from the inside which is something that is impossible for natural scientists. On the other hand, there is the sceptical tradition instanced by the logical positivists and Marxists as well as inductivists. For this group, the fact that we share language with our objects of study is the source of great problems associated with the achievement and maintenance of accurate observation or objectivity. This is because, whatever its scientific content, language is also the carrier of preconceptions, values and therefore sympathies and interests which can be the sources of bias. As a result it is considered to be an untrustworthy medium for both investigation and analysis. Language is therefore best approached in one of two ways. First, in the empiricist manner by attempting to subordinate it to vision even more firmly through stressing the scientific primacy of observation and moving as quickly as possible into the realm of numbers and statistics. Second, by approaching any linguistic phenomena with an ideological health warning in mind such as Marx's famous dictum that the 'the ideas of the ruling class are in every epoch the ruling ideas' (Marx and Engels, 1970, p. 64).

In sum, and despite the various suggestions of a more complex relationship just indicated, for sociologists our sharing of language with our objects of study has been considered as either a good thing because it allows access to social truth or a bad thing because it can obscure such truth. Unfortunately, the former position has affected sociological sight by tending to dissolve any concept of social structure, while the latter has affected it by tending to exclude the cultural realm from its conception of social structure. That is, despite various suggestions to the contrary, the capacity of language and the social conditions in which it is embedded to affect theoretical vision has not been considered as a topic of reflexive methodological concern in its own right.

In my view, this is because, largely unknowingly, sociologists have been committed, at least formally, to an understanding of the nature of language which is derived from the vision-dependent representationalist paradigm. According to this understanding, words in themselves are the neutral, symbolic means that human beings use to picture or re-present and so communicate their ideas concerning things and actions in the world to one another (see the central vertical flow line in Figure 1). If this communication is biased in any way, it is because either, as for the Neo-Kantian tradition, this is because of the unavoidable partiality of individuals or, as for the empiricist and Marxist traditions, this is necessarily the case where science does not govern common sense. Thus language use is understood to be part of a larger visuality in that it is thought to operate either at the behest of the subjects using or of the society producing it. However, language in itself is regarded as immune to the effects of any such larger visuality.

In the Neo-Kantian case, one may speak of a rationalist variant of representationalism because language is understood to

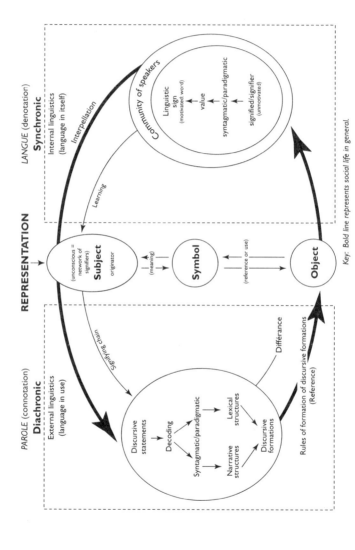

Figure 1 From representation to signification

apply pre-existing mental pictures of things or actions to those things or actions in the world. Such is the attraction of this variety of representationalism that, for many phenomenological and symbolic interactionist readers at least, it overwhelmed the suggestions to the contrary contained in the inaugural statements of these positions by figures such as Weber and Charles Sanders Pierce. In the sceptical case, one may speak of an empiricist variant in that language is simply a way of reporting to the mind how things are, largely on the basis of what they look like and despite the contrary intuition that this may be simply a societal effect. In whatever form, representationalism's vision-dependence rules out the need to specify the mechanisms of sight and language with the result that Sociology generally understands language and therefore the cultural, ideological and theoretical things that live within it to lack any inherent autonomy or any independent, socially or intellectually determinative capacity as social life forms.

As it turns out, it is surprising and unfortunate that sociologists should have refused to problematise the vision-dependence of their conceptions of language for so long after much of the rest of the academic world had taken up the new conception created by the paradigm shift produced by Ferdinand de Saussure's inauguration of Structural Linguistics. Before I explain why this refusal now seems surprising and is also unfortunate, I will briefly explain what Saussure's revolution involved. It began with the rejection of the search for origins and the consequent vision dependency that had dominated Linguistics for much of its history. Instead, Saussure proposed that language should not be thought of as the product of human beings who supposedly saw before they spoke but in the first instance as simply an eternal property of the social relations that make speech possible and therefore affect what we see (see the right-hand side of Figure 1; the left-hand side is explicated below pp. 153–6). For Saussure, then, language's critical components are those that make it possible (*langue*) rather than those that give it expression (*parole*), and those that account for its stability (synchronic relations) rather than for its transformation (diachronic relations). In order to describe the core of *langue*'s synchronic relations, Saussure disinterred the ancient Stoic vocabulary for analysing language and spoke of it as comprising 'signifiers' (sets of sound differences or impressions) and 'signifieds' (sets of mental or conceptual differences or impressions). These are given value or meaning through being brought into alignment with one another to form signs (words) by the operation of syntagmatic relations (the rules of syntax, for example) and associative or paradigmatic relations (lexicons).

THE SIGNIFICANCE OF STRUCTURAL LINGUISTICS

The negative consequences of all this for representationalism are threefold and have great significance for how we are now able to understand the limitations and possibilities of theoretical work and therefore to conceptualise social structure which will gradually become apparent as the present text proceeds. First, possessed of this inner motor, so to speak, and therefore governed by a specific ecology, language and therefore the cultural or discursive things that exist within it possess an irreducible if necessarily incomplete autonomy that makes them permanently capable of escaping from the control of both subjects and other social processes. And it is because this autonomy creates a tiny sphere of freedom and therefore danger for human beings in general and theorists in particular in that it imposes a reflexive methodological responsibility – are the particular concepts used the product of the larger set consciously deployed, which is what they should be, or do they come from other mental structures such as common sense or political ideology? Second, not only is the connection between signifiers and signifieds arbitrary in the sense that neither determines what the other must be, but also therefore the relationship between signs and the things and actions in the world to which they refer must be arbitrary too. That is, a word including a theoretical term cannot exist on its own and as a meaningful entity as a picture or representation of the world. Instead it can only exist as an element in a much larger system of picturing or representing the world, of giving it meaning. Or again, language is not composed of pictures of the world but instead is a means of picturing or representing it that as such is at least partially governed by processes and mechanisms intrinsic to itself which owe nothing to the world external to it.

However, third, because of the arbitrariness of the relations between signs and their extra-linguistic referents, an under-standing of *langue* alone cannot tell us why its users in fact take words to refer to certain specific things and actions in the world and not simply certain ideas or descriptions of them. In Saussure's own and too little noticed words:

the arbitrariness of language radically separates it from all other institutions. This is apparent from the way in which lan-guage evolves. Nothing could be more complex. As it is a product of both the social force and time, no one can change anything in it, and on the other hand, the arbitrariness of its signs theoretically entails the freedom of establishing just any relationship between phonetic substance and ideas. The result is that each of the two elements united in a sign maintains its own life to a degree unknown elsewhere, and that language changes, or rather evolves, under the influence of all the forces which can effect either sounds or meanings. The evolution is inevitable; there is no example of a single language that resists it. After a certain period of time, some obvious shifts can always be recorded (Saussure, 1974, p. 76).

Thus to understand linguistic change and therefore by extension to understand linguistic and theoretical reference requires much more than an understanding of the structures and processes intrinsic to *langue*. What this 'much more' involves, the imbrication of language with social life in general to form visualities, will be discussed at length in Chapter 4, as will the reflexive methodological freedom and consequent responsibility that is granted to and imposed upon the theorist by language's incomplete autonomy.

If it now seems surprising that sociologists did not more quickly shift to Saussure's significatory paradigm, it is because a critical source of inspiration for Saussure as he reformulated what Linguistics should be about was Emile Durkheim's insistence on the *sui generis* character of social relations. Indeed it was noting this point alongside their far from common-sensical envisionings of the social that prompted me to investigate the possibility that not only Durkheim but perhaps also Marx and Weber too might in fact have worked with a different even if unconscious understanding of the nature of language and therefore of what is involved in theoretical envisioning to those which they consciously espoused (see Chapter 1 for the positive results of this investigation). It is also unfortunate that sociologists did not more quickly make this shift because by the time some attempted to do so the consequences for the understanding of visuality and therefore reference had been forgotten and Saussure's ideas had been transformed by many philosophers and literary critics into Humpty Dumpty-like claims for the absolute and entirely internally generated referential power and autonomy of linguistic and cultural processes more generally (see pp. 155–7 below).

The implications of what has been said so far, which will also be further spelt out and justified as the text proceeds, are as follows. First, any theoretical enterprise that depends upon the vision-dependent, rationalistic representationalism is necessarily intellectually anachronistic. Second, it is therefore also likely to be ignorant of what might be termed its own natural history and therefore of its limitations. Third, as Nietzsche and Durkheim suggest in the epigraphs with which this text begins, the results of such anachronistic activity are likely to be intellectually and indeed politically banal in that they are unlikely to be anything other than more sophisticated repetitions of the common sense of the day. Fourth, and this time positively, the proper reflexive acknowledgement of the linguistic and discursive nature of social theory would constitute an event of equivalent significance to that of the marginalist revolution in Economics which, misleadingly, ended in the naming of the paradigmatic mode of that discipline as 'Neo-Classicism'. In the sociological case I would suggest that the label neo-classical is

13

far more appropriate since the paradigm shift to which it refers is one that the classical authors themselves achieved, albeit unconsciously and incompletely. What makes the use of the term misleading with respect to economics is the fact that the marginalist revolution reworked the discipline on the basis of ontological and methodological individualism (Wagner, 1994, p. 108) which is a particularly impoverished instance of the consequences of rationalist representationalism. By contrast, my argument will be that the Saussurian revolution suggests that Sociology at least should be revisualised on the basis of an ontological and methodological sociologism derived from the work of the classical authors since it is only then that we will once again be able to see beyond those visible dimensions of the social that are embodied in individual and corporate actions.

Jacques Derrida reminds us somewhere that the preface is always the last part of a book to be completed. Thus, despite the appearance to the contrary, a preface does not represent a starting point from whence the remainder rationally unfolds. Rather, it represents an ending in that it distils what was learnt in the course of writing. It is for this reason as well as its programmatic nature that the present text as a whole should be understood as a preface, albeit rather a long one. This is because it is an attempt to describe or distil a starting point for a neo-classical sociology that has long been present in my mind as a kind of metatheoretical imago as I have taught and written. Another reason is that I hope that the reader will allow me to take advantage of the prefatory form and so argue in an assertive, selective and lightly referenced way, since much of the detailed support for what I will have to say as well as its development and application is contained in earlier theoretical and substantive writings around the themes of production, law, class and human rights which it would be tiresome for all concerned for me to repeat. However, immodestly, I have not been shy to point out by my self-referencing where at least some of this previous work is pertinent to the issues discussed.

AN ORDINARY REALIST METATHEORY

Since most of what follows is devoted to the recommendation of an only partially new metatheoretical basis for social theory in that I propose reworking it on the basis of the non-vision-dependent, significatory conception of language, I had better make clear at the outset what my other and more traditional metatheoretical presuppositions are. Ontologically, I am a realist in that I am committed to the view that the world, including the social world, is best approached by assuming that it subsists independently of our thought about it. For this reason I am also necessarily a materialist since if the world were not accessible through our senses there would be no grounds for assuming its externality to our minds. As indicated above, my final ontological assumption is that, for Sociology at least, the world is to be understood as composed of structural entities and their interactions rather than of human beings. The latter are self-evidently a social presence and they clearly affect what happens in society (Woodiwiss, 1990a, pp. 25–7, 72–3, 153–5). However, they are not the only presence since non-human subjects or corporate bodies of one kind or another are also present. These corporate bodies cannot be understood as the simple aggregations of human wills since they are only

15

possible because of the existence of certain political, economic, discursive and often legal preconditions too, which, in turn, also cannot be understood in terms of human action alone since they are the conditions of possibility for one another whether or not actors are aware of them.

My strategic reason, then, for insisting in the current context that at the most fundamental level the social world consists of non-human structural entities and the relations between them is not that they are the only things that exist in society, but rather that they have tended to be rendered invisible when necessarily visible subjects of whatever kind are taken as the atoms of sociality. That is, following Durkheim and the structuralist tradition more generally, I believe that the primary task of Sociology is to make visible the preconditional structures themselves and their interactions. This is a task that seems to be simply impossible if one works with a humanist ontology even though, of course, one must pay attention to what human beings and other actors do, since their activities contain evidence for the existence of and transformations within other more strictly social life forms. It is puzzling in a way that we have not got further with the realisation of the Durkheimian project. Although the latter is by no means a simple undertaking, the tasks of understanding the limits to and effects of human action seem even more complex to me, not least because they require a background knowledge of social structure and individual psyches that we simply do not have and in the case of the latter should not anyway place in the public domain.

For me, then, and for reasons that have much to do with Sociology's unknowing representationalism, we have too often put the cart of understanding human action before the horse of understanding social structure. To be clear, I say this not because I have an 'over-socialised' conception of human beings as 'cultural dopes' or whatever. I have too much respect for the conscious and unconscious powers of the human mind to accept such an idea (see Craib, 1990). Instead, it is purely because I think we should attend to the 'simpler' task first, not least because attempts to explain human actions on the basis of seriously incomplete understandings of the social-structural contexts within which they are located are likely to be a waste of time. And this despite the extraordinary amount of intellectual effort and creativity they require and the pleasure they may consequently give to their producers and consumers.

Before moving on to say something very brief about my epistemological presuppositions, I should make one final clarificatory point concerning the nature of my ontological realism. This is that I am what might be termed an 'ordinary realist' or what Roy Bhaskar (1978) used to call a 'scientific realist' (see also, Boyd et al., 1991; Hacking, 1983). I therefore do not subscribe to what Bhaskar (1989) now calls 'critical realism'. Inspired in part by Jürgen Habermas, what Bhaskar appears to mean by critical realism is as follows. Whereas the non-human world in no way depends upon us thinking about it for its existence and is therefore to be understood as an 'intransitive' dimension of being, the human and especially the social world is so dependent, at least in part, and is therefore 'transitive' as well as 'intransitive'. For this reason he concludes that, because the thoughts and actions of social scientists can affect the nature of the social world in a way that they cannot affect the nature of the non-human world, we ought to be committed to the removal of the sources of social injustice.

17

I wholly agree with the goal of removing the sources of social injustice, and I even agree that this is a legitimate goal for a social scientist to subscribe to. However, what I cannot agree with is Bhaskar's argument that what makes such commitment follow from one's scientific work is the difference between the social world and the non-human world. This is for two reasons. First, as explained above, I do not agree that social structure should be ontologically distinguished from the non-human world – to believe that social structure as distinguished from social life in general both depends on us thinking about it for its existence and does not so depend is either self-contradictory – now it is, now it is not – or no position at all rather than the route to what some refer to as a 'rich and complex ontology'. Indeed for this reason I consider myself to be a much more rigorous naturalist than Bhaskar whom I fear at this point falls prey to representationalism and therefore compromises with Neo-Kantianism and so contradicts his own avowal of realism. Second, I do not think that scientific work provides an at all adequate basis for moral or political commitments, which on the contrary are more appropriately grounded in experience or, in its absence, a knowledge of ethical and political discourses which of course may and probably should be articulated with one's scientific work. On this issue, if few others, I agree with Jean Francois Lyotard (see below, pp. 135–138) when he argues that we should fear the moral arrogance of any science. However, to argue that social science is an insufficient basis for politics does not mean that social science in itself has no political significance. Of course it has and I will endeavour to point out both why this should be the case and what this significance might be at several points in the main body of what follows.

All that said, despite my serious ontological differences with the later Bhaskar, I am in full agreement with him as regards epistemology. That is, I agree and have always been guided in my practice by the alternative to empiricism that he outlines: namely, observation should be theory-driven; causal-modelling and testing are better means of articulating theory and data than hypothesis testing for generalisations; and, because of the irreducible difference between our minds and what they seek to comprehend, results are always ultimately fallible rather than ever certainly explain even part of what empiricists term the 'variance' (see also, Alexander's [1982, pp. 30–3] specification of 'postpositivism'). So much for my metatheoretical position, except that much of what follows is an elaboration of and attempt to justify what has just been said. Metatheoretical statements and perhaps especially those pertaining to ontology, are prefaces too since, far from being arbitrary, they represent a certain way of summarising one's scientific experience. I will conclude, then, with an account of how the present text reformulates my experience as a narrative.

Chapter 1 reviews the recent debate concerning the supposed canonical status of Marx, Weber and Durkheim, and finds that it has been conducted in an unhelpfully moralistic register. It then moves on to consider whether the work of the classical theorists might nonetheless be anachronistic on account of the vision-dependent nature of their theoretical practice. A close reading of their texts is undertaken which demonstrates that each of them in fact achieved a non-vision-dependent and therefore non-representationalist mode of theorising which is what both explains and justifies a conception of the sociological future as neo-classical. Chapter 2 engages in another set of close readings and shows that Tom Marshall and David Lockwood sustained the classical achievement, while Anthony Giddens and Stuart Hall were forced to neglect it as a consequence of their regression to vision.

Chapter 3 argues that the return of representationalism and therefore the privileging of vision to social theory through the work of Giddens, Hall and regrettably many others too has had very negative consequences for more substantive sociological understandings. These are summarised by the current omnipresence of the term 'modernity' as a general descriptor of social structures which is not only myopically Ameri-centric but requires us to forget still more of what the classical theorists taught us about the nature of sociality. Chapter 4 begins with an account of Postmodernism and its attractions before moving on to show how Martin Jay's differentiation of scopic regimes enables one to resist this particular siren. It ends by suggesting that in his now unjustly neglected masterpiece, *The Archaeology of Knowledge*, Michel Foucault not only provided a sociological theory of discursive and therefore theoretical reference but also a non-representationalist and realist basis for a social science, a metatheoretical visuality, that surpasses the pre-existing visualities and therefore provides a rigorous starting point for the reworking of social theory.

The Conclusion begins by repeating the two rules of neo-classical method produced by the argumentation of the preceding chapters. These are:

It is a necessary but not a sufficient condition of non-representationalist theoretical development that it is undertaken in the context of substantive research.

Theoretical discourses that are wholly a product of a representationalist theoretical practice should be discarded, while those that are not, or at least not entirely, the product of such a practice may be retained either as they are or for reworking.

It then moves on to show how these two rules could help us to recover the understanding of social structure that we have lost. It also exemplifies the still very substantial shortcomings of this understanding by reference to its orientalist character. And finally, it both identifies the means by which neo-classical reasoning may be able to overcome such limitations and demonstrates how this might be done by producing a theorisation of globalisation as a social fact which arises out of my ongoing substantive work in the area of human rights.

21

CHAPTER ONE

From Vision to Visuality in Classical Social Theory

Within at least the Sociology departments of Britain and North America, and usually prompted by self-described Postmodernists or their allies, a sometimes rather fierce debate has raged over the 'core' status of the classical writers for the past ten years or so, often with far-reaching consequences for the curriculum. However, despite their political successes in many departments, little of much weight has been published on the issue by the Postmodernist side until recently.

Although I am not at all sure that he would describe himself as a postmodernist, the critique of the foundational status of the classics by the Australian sociologist, Bob Connell (1997), articulates a sophisticated version of the postmodernist argument (see also, Turner, 1996). The starting point of Connell's argument is the claim that the classical authors constitute a 'canon' in the now current literary sense of the term; that is, 'a privileged set of texts, whose interpretation and reinterpretation defines a field' (ibid., p. 1512). This he considers puzzling for two main reasons. First, much of quantitative sociology totally ignores the classical writings even as a source of possible hypotheses. Second, the other sociologists of the formative period did not ascribe any special status to Marx, Weber or Durkheim, whether considered alone or together. In fact, Connell states, it was not until the publication of Talcott Parsons's *The Structure of Social Action* in 1937 that an argument for such status was made. What the recognition of the late date of formation of the canon calls for in Connell's view is a new look at the history of the discipline in order to understand both what sociologists thought it was about before they were told it was what was defined by the classics and why the latter were selected. On the first score Connell finds that the discipline did not focus on the endogenous development of the West as post-canon historians of the discipline like Nisbet (1967) have so influentially argued. Rather, Connell's extensive survey of nineteenth-century, non-classical sociological writings suggests to him that the understanding and management of the territories acquired in the course of Western colonial and imperial expansion would be a more accurate account of the actual focus of interest. Thus he sees nineteenth- and early twentieth-century sociology as a discourse of superiority, thematised as 'Progress', which focused on issues of 'race' and gender, deployed the ethnographic and comparative methods of the 'Imperial Gaze', and obscured the violence of the colonial encounter.

In Connell's view, the serenity of the 'Imperial Gaze' was shattered by the explosion of imperial rivalries that resulted in the First World War. He continues that the fact that this dreadful event was forced on the world by the supposedly most advanced nations destroyed the sociological belief in 'Progress', and at last the discipline turned inwards, so to speak. This was especially the case in the United States, where the emergence of the Chicago School in the 1920s resulted in the reorientation of the discipline around the largely untheorised theme of 'social control'. Interest in theory slowly revived in the 1940s and 1950s as sociology became a popular subject in the emerging mass higher education system and therefore needed a more sophisticated intellectual rationale. This was the need met by Parsons, C. Wright Mills and the other classical buffs. Connell sees two major problems with the intellectual legacy resulting from this history: the continuation of the silence concerning the violence of the colonial encounter and the addition of a new silence concerning 'race' and gender. His solution to the problems resulting from these silences is that we should learn to live without the classics and draw inspiration instead from the pluralism of nineteenth-century sociology if not from its content.

In his riposte, Randall Collins (1997) challenges most of Connell's substantive assertions concerning the discipline's history and rejects what he terms his 'guilt tripping' approach. He counters by arguing that nineteenth-century Sociology was in fact significantly concerned with endogenous Western development, was not always patronising in its discussions of non-Western societies, and deployed the comparative method more because of the inspiration of the natural sciences, notably biology, than because of the exigencies informing any 'Imperial Gaze'. He also suggests that nineteenth-century sociologists had more interest in sexuality than 'race' and gender *per se*. Moreover, he argues that Connell's canon is a specifically American construct that has never been accepted in France and Germany, for example, where national champions and traditions have retained their privileged positions. Finally, in Collins's view the classical canon was constructed to challenge empiricism rather than to legitimate it.

To my mind there is something wrong with the whole register of this debate in that it is conducted in evaluative rather than analytical terms. For the most part we are asked to consider whether or not the classics are good for us as human beings rather than whether or not they are useful to us as sociologists. Although neither Connell nor Collins appear to be aware of this, this skewing of the nature of their debate is the rhetorical effect of the former's casual and unchallenged use of the term canon to refer to the classical writings. The predictability of this consequence is made very clear in the source Connell gives for his use of the term. There, we read the following:

the 'canonizers' of early Christianity were not concerned with how beautiful texts were, nor with how universal their appeal might be. They acted with a very clear concept of how texts would 'measure up' to the standards of their religious community, or conform to their 'rule'. They were concerned above all else with distinguishing the orthodox from the heretical.

In recent years many literary critics have become convinced that the selection of literary texts for 'canonisation' (the selection of what are conventionally called the 'classics') operates in a way very like the formation of the biblical canon. These critics detect beneath the supposed objectivity of value judgements a political agenda: the exclusion of many groups of people from representation in the literary canon (Guillory, 1995, p. 233).

Clearly, then, the term canon is replete with evaluative connotations. Hence the virtually automatic tendency for the debates in which it figures to result in the trading of denunciations, as in the case of the recent American 'culture wars' around the issue of multiculturalism and the content of introductory literature courses in particular. Sidestepping the issue of the appropriateness or otherwise of the use of the term in the literary context – except to say that its rhetorical effects appear to have made it harder for both sides to do justice to their respective positions – the question I wish to pose is: 'Was the process of selection out of which the sociological classics emerged primarily a moral and/or political one?'. Without for one minute denying the sins of Sociology's past and present, nor even the production of certain exclusionary effects consequent on the particular character of the classics, it is very clear to me that the process of selection was primarily neither moral nor political. Specifically, it is extremely clear that, whether one agrees with them of not, Parsons' reasons in respect of the choice of Weber and Durkheim's texts as classics were overwhelmingly technical and analytical (see below, pp. 65–68). Again, my point is not to deny that analytical choices have either moral/political determinants or consequences but simply to assert the rather simple proposition that they are different and therefore can be discussed and indeed related without being reduced to one another.

What might the technical and analytical reasons be for the selection of texts by Weber, Durkheim and, latterly, Marx as constitutive of the discipline's core? Alexander (1987) gives a very detailed and closely argued account of what at least some of them might be in a piece published ten years earlier than Connell's and indeed referred to by him. Alexander is concerned to defend the role of the classics *vis-à-vis* the scepticism of the sociological empiricists whose battle cry remains Alfred North Whitehead's famous dictum: 'A science that hesitates to forget its founders is lost'. Nevertheless, interestingly, much of his argument is just as relevant to the postmodernist challenge because both groups seem to be equally immodestly unaware of the debts they owe to the bearded ones. One of Alexander's most general points is that, because Sociology is a non-paradigmatic science in Kuhn's sense, its practitioners require as a practical necessity a shorthand way of referring to their differences while being able to continue not only to work in their plural ways but also to be able to communicate across the barriers that divide them. This is what precisely the *differences* between Marx, Weber and Durkheim provided and provide for many if not, of course, all sociologists. Developing this idea, Alexander then goes on to summarise the analytical reasons behind their special position by referring to the creative stimulation they have provided within the discipline since the ending of the Second World War, whether in their own right, through the tensions between them, or because of efforts to dislodge them from their pre-eminent positions.

If one accepts Alexander's points, as I do, but at the same time does not wish to deny that Sociology is as much a system of power/knowledge as any other discipline, one needs to find an alternative concept to that of the canon with which to think through the problem – if that is what it is – represented by the classics. For reasons that will be more fully explained in Chapter 4 I consider the Foucaldian concepts of discursive formation and rules of formation to be the best available alternative. For now I will restrict myself to providing a substantive rather than an analytical reason why I feel confident about

27

refusing to engage in a more detailed contestation of Connell's moralistic argument (but see below, pp. 158–61). As Foucault's disciplinary histories make clear, all of them have their criminal pasts. However, for example, no one suggests that we should do without the knowledge of the functioning of the body's internal organs that was gained as a result of body-snatching.

For the present I am principally interested in the simpler matter of the resistance to changes in the objects of analysis produced by representationalism. Basically, this resistance occurs because representationalism of whatever kind tends to fix for all time what concepts can be made to refer to because it pictures them at a particular time and place. Thus the question that I wish to pose to the texts of the classical authors is: 'Are their theories inherently representationalist?' If the answer is positive, it seems that those who wish us to forget them are correct. If the answer is negative, it seems that there are grounds for retaining and, if necessary, reworking them. And finally, if the answer is part positive and part negative, it means that we should have a good idea of how they might be reconstructed or augmented so that they are more capable of responding to changes within the sphere of objects.

REPRESENTATIONALISM AND ITS OTHER IN MARX

Marx's writings provide few signs that he knew much in detail about the representationalist Linguistics of his day let alone had any critical thoughts about it. Nevertheless, they do make it clear that he shared the educated person's grasp of what the

linguists were arguing.[1] Thus, although his writings are silent
about the achievements of the French Grammarian tradition
that crystallised at Port Royal towards the end of the seventeenth century, they display explicit support for the then
current privileging of phonology and the argument of the
comparative philologists that languages developed in sophistication with their host societies. Thus his two comments on
language in *The Economic and Philosophical Manuscripts* of 1844
are as follows:

> But also when I am active *scientifically*, etc. – when I am
> engaged in activity that which I can seldom perform in direct
> community with others – then I am *social*, because I am
> active as a *man*. Not only is the material of my activity given
> to me as a social product (as is even the language in which the
> thinker is active): my *own* existence *is* social activity (Marx,
> 1964, p. 137, emphasis in original).

> *nature* is the immediate object of the *science of man*: the
> first object of man – man – is nature, sensuousness [that
> which is accessible to the senses, A.W.]; and the particular
> sensuous human essential powers can only find their self-
> understanding in the science of the natural world in general,
> since they can find their objective realisation in *natural*
> objects only. The element of thought itself – the element of
> thought's living expression – *language* – is of a sensuous
> nature. The *social* reality of nature, and *human natural science*,
> or the natural science *about man*, are identical terms (ibid.,
> p. 143, emphasis in original).

These commitments plus his own philosophical temper meant that, even if he had known about them, he would have had little or no sympathy with the Romanticist ideas about language associated with such figures as Giambattista Vico and Wilhelm von Humbolt. These were ideas that increased in popularity as the nineteenth century progressed and in one way or another suggested the potentially anti-representationalist thesis that language could be as determinant of thought as reality. However, for Marx they would have been part and parcel of the legacy of the Hegelianism against which he respectfully defined his position. Thus he and Friedrich Engels deploy the empiricist variant of the representationalist conception of language against the Hegelians in *The German Ideology*:

> man also possesses 'consciousness', but, even so, not inherent, not 'pure' consciousness. From the start the 'spirit' is afflicted with the curse of being 'burdened' with matter, which here makes its appearance in the form of agitated layers of air, sounds, in short, of language. *Language is as old as consciousness, language is practical consciousness that exists also for other men, and for that reason alone it really exists for me personally as well*; language, like consciousness, only arises from the need, the necessity of intercourse with other men. Where there exists a relationship, it exists for me: the animal does not enter into 'relations' with anything, it does not enter into any relation at all. For the animal, its relation to others does not exist as a relation. Consciousness is, therefore, from the very beginning a social product, and remains so as long as men exist at all (Marx and Engels, 1970, pp. 50–1, emphasis added).

Or again:

> For philosophers, one of the most difficult tasks is to descend
> from the world of thought to the actual world. *Language* is
> the immediate actuality of thought. Just as philosophers have
> given thought an independent existence, so they had to make
> language into an independent realm. This is the secret of
> philosophical language, in which thoughts in the form of
> words have their own content. The problem of descending
> from the world of thoughts to the actual world is turned into
> the problem of descending from language to life . . . . The
> philosophers would only have to dissolve their language
> into the ordinary language, from which it is abstracted, to
> recognise it as the distorted language of the actual world, and
> to realise that neither thoughts nor language in themselves
> form a realm of their own, that they are only *manifestations* of
> actual life (ibid., p. 491, emphasis in the original).

In sum, as he says earlier: 'Philosophy and the study of the
actual world have the same relation to one another as masturbation and sexual love' (ibid., p. 103). However, as the second
of the longer passages suggests, there is a tension in Marx's
work between his conviction as to the basically representationalist character of language and his equally strong conviction that
it is a social product. This latter conviction means that language
can be used to distort the nature of what it represents. It is this
tension, then, that enabled him to produce in *Capital, I* the justly
famous complication of the empiricist variant of the representationalist problematic that constitutes the most developed
form of his theory of ideology, namely his concept of the

'fetishism of commodities' that for him so distorts perception in capitalist societies:

> There is a definite social relation between men, that assumes, in their eyes, the fantastic form of a relation between things. In order therefore to find an analogy, we must have recourse to the mist-enveloped regions of the religious world. In that world the productions of the human brain appear as independent beings endowed with life, and entering into relation both with one another and the human race. So it is in the world of commodities with the products of men's hands. This I call the Fetishism which attaches itself to the products of labour, so soon as they are produced as commodities, and which is therefore inseparable from the production of commodities (Marx, 1867, p. 72).

In case the significance of this passage for the nature of Marx's understanding of language is not clear enough, I will provide a quotation from the earlier *German Ideology* in which Marx both shows that the idea of the fetishism of commodities had been with him for some time before he came to write *Capital* and displays his understanding of the role of language within the mechanism that it represents:

> For the bourgeois it is so much the easier to prove on the basis of his language, the identity of the commercial and the individual, or even universal, human relations, since this language is itself a product of the bourgeoisie, and therefore in actuality as in language the relations of buying and selling have been made the basis of all others (Marx and Engels, 1970. p. 247).

All that said, it is important not to think that because Marx consciously complicated the representationalist problematic he escaped from it either easily or knowingly. Indeed in all his work prior to the *Grundrisse* of 1857 he appears to have been assertively representationalist in the empiricist mode since he clearly thought that the best antidote for philosophical masturbation was the accurate verbal depiction of reality. Thus, as he says in the preface to *The Economic and Philosophical Manuscripts*, 'my results have been attained by means of a wholly empirical analysis', and later, '[s]ense-perception ... must be the basis of all science' (ibid., p. 143). A good example of the representationalist character of his empirical analysis may be found at the opening of the first chapter, the 'Wages of Labour':

> Wages are determined through the antagonistic struggle between capitalist and worker. Victory goes necessarily to the capitalist. The capitalist can live longer without the worker than can the worker without the capitalist. Combination among capitalists is customary and effective; worker's combination is prohibited and painful in its consequences for them (ibid., p. 65).

The representationalism of this passage resides in the fact that not one term in this the fundamental thesis of the manuscripts signifies anything that is not in principle visible and therefore observable. Of course Marx continues the passage from the preface quoted earlier by adding that his wholly empirical analysis is 'based on a conscientious critical study of political economy'. However, from the text it is clear that Marx regarded the concepts of political economy, 'profits' and 'wages' in particular, as accurate but incomplete depictions of capitalist economic reality. What is required is an understanding of their 'connection' (ibid., p. 167) that is not derived from some 'fictitious primordial condition' (ibid.) but is an 'economic fact of the present'; to wit:

> the object that labour produces . . . confronts it as *something alien*, as power *independent* of the producer. The product of labour is labour which has become material: it is the *objectification* of labour. Labour's realisation is its objectification. In the sphere of political economy this realisation of labour appears as *loss of realisation* for the workers; objectification as *loss of the object* as *bondage* to it; appropriation as *estrangement*, as *alienation* (ibid., p. 108, emphasis in the original).

As Marx says on the following page, 'political economy *conceals* the estrangement inherent in the nature of labour' (emphasis added) and therefore he makes a strenuous effort in the passage just cited precisely to picture it. Restated to bring out its representationalism, the passage may be read as follows: alienation occurs where the product of labour becomes objectified, something material and therefore something visible that can be taken away from the labourer who thereafter is in bondage to that which he or she can see but not retain.

Marx's commitment to representationalism is especially emphatically stated in the opening chapter of *The German Ideology* where we find:

> This method of approach is not devoid of premises. It starts out from real premises and does not abandon them for a

moment. Its premises are men, not in any fantastic isolation
and rigidity, but in their actual, empirically perceptible
process of development under definite conditions
   Where the speculation ends – in real life – there real,
positive science begins: the representation of the practical
... development of men .... When reality is *depicted*,
philosophy as an independent branch of knowledge loses
its medium of existence (Marx and Engels, 1970, p. 48,
emphasis added).

Given the strength of his metatheoretical commitment to
representationalism, it is not at all surprising that Marx's
historical and political works are so pictorialist in character,
especially the remarkable *tableau vivant* that is the *Communist
Manifesto*, wherein the classes are presented as straightfor-
wardly real actors who have done battle with one another
down the ages.
   That said, there was a rationalist spectre haunting Marx,
a ghost in his mental machine, that he both enjoyed 'coquetting'
(Marx, 1867, p. 20) with and continuously drew inspiration
from, namely Hegel. Thus, although he tried very hard to
turn Hegelian rationalist representations like the dialectic and
alienation into picturable empirical facts, he seems to have been
continuously challenged by an agonistically produced intuition
concerning the possibility that somewhere there existed what
he eventually referred to as the 'hidden abode of production':
an abode that was so deeply hidden as to be unrepresentable or
undepictable in an empirical sense: 'in the analysis of economic
forms neither *microscopes* nor chemical reagents are of use. The
force of abstraction must replace both' (Marx, 1867, p. 8,

emphasis added). It is this intuition, or so it seems to me, that in continuing tension with his fierce commitment to empiricist representationalism produced both the extraordinary intellectual energy and the frustration apparent in his various efforts to write what eventually became *Capital*: specifically in the *Grundrisse*, the *Preface* and *Introduction to a Critique of Political Economy*, and the *Theories of Surplus Value*. As Terrell Carver (1975, p. 38) has put it:

> The most striking difference between the *Introduction* [*Grundrisse*] and Marx's earlier and later writings was his overt interest in the logical interrelations of the concepts and categories of political economy. He pursued that sort of investigation at length . . . confident that he was not falling into any idealist traps

The eventual overcoming of this tension also accounts for the pleasure that Marx takes in the form of volume one of *Capital* where the first six chapters follow the narrative structure of a conjuring act: first we are reassured that everything is as normal but suddenly a rabbit is produced – Marx's version of the labour theory of value. Thus in Chapter 1 we are presented with a picture of the world as we commonly experience it but warned that all is not what it seems – human relationships are hidden behind those between things thanks to the fetishism of commodities. In Chapter 2 he describes the typical form that human relationships take in such a world, namely relations of exchange. In Chapter 3 Marx states that as a result the typical medium through which human relationships take place is money. In Chapter 4 he points out that once money appears an

additional form of the circulation of commodities also appears –
money is invested in commodities to become money again, only
this time its quantum has increased. In Chapter 5 he feigns
disbelief at this outcome and wonders if it is the result of
'magic', since on the surface at least all exchanges are exchanges
of equivalents. In Chapter 6, he finally pulls the rabbit out
of the hat:

> In order to be able to extract value from the consumption of
> a commodity, our friend, Moneybags, must be so lucky as to
> find, within the sphere of circulation, in the market, a com-
> modity whose use-value possesses the peculiar property of
> being a source of value, whose actual consumption, there-
> fore, is itself an embodiment of labour, and, consequently, a
> creation of value. The possessor of money does find on the
> market such a special commodity in capacity for labour or
> labour-power.
>
> By labour-power or capacity for labour is to be under-
> stood the aggregate of those mental and physical capabilities
> existing in a human being, which he exercises whenever he
> produces a use-value of any description (*Capital*, vol.1,
> p. 167).

As Marx says at the end of the chapter:

> Accompanied by Mr Moneybags and by the possessor of
> labour-power, we therefore take leave for a time of this noisy
> sphere, where everything takes place on the surface and in
> the view of all men, and follow them into the hidden abode
> of production (ibid., p. 176).

In conceptual terms too Marx enters new territory since the theoretical apparatus necessary to bring the hidden abode and its significance to light evokes such unpicturable processes and entities as the extraction of various forms of 'surplus value', the 'mode of production' and, eventually, the 'tendency of the rate of profit to fall'.

The net result for Marx's conception of theory was, as Carver (1975, p. 133) again has put it, using quotes from the *Grundrisse*:

> In Marx's work, concepts may be said to exist only in man's thoughts, speech, and written language; concepts are very much man's products, and any development of them is traceable to man, not to 'Spirit', the 'Idea' or the 'concept thinking outside or above [human] perception and conceptualisation'. Marx concludes that the 'method of ascending from the abstract to the concrete is merely the way of thinking to appropriate the concrete, to reproduce it as a mental concrete'.

In *Capital*, then, not only is conceptual elaboration far more important than description in a quantitative sense than in any of Marx's earlier published work, but also this theorising refers to processes and entities that are neither visible in themselves nor in their inter-connections. Instead of theory being a picture or set of pictures of the world as in the *Manuscripts*, it has become an inter-related set of conceptual signs which makes the social picturable – as summarised by Marx's famous architectural metaphor of base and superstructure. In sum, vision has been replaced by a consciously constructed visuality as the means of representing the world and this visuality was both more purely significatory than that informing the fetishism of commodities and very different from Hegel's.

In many ways, of course, the location of such a break in Marx's thought is only a development of Althusser's point about there being an epistemological break between the younger ontologically humanist Marx and the older non-humanist Marx. Indeed, although I do not share Althusser's obsession with the precise location of the break, I nevertheless feel that our two arguments reinforce one another because of the reciprocal inter-connections between the various metatheoretical elements (see below, pp. 140–1). Thus I agree with Althusser that the concepts Marx developed earlier in his career are more problematic than those he developed later. An example is the concept of class which because it was developed early and extensively deployed in Marx's historical writings has a very strong representationalist content which currently appears to threaten the concept's very existence in the contemporary sociological lexicon. Thus, now that the British working class is no longer personified by people of a particular gender, ethnicity, proportion of the population or taste in headgear, some sociologists (Pahl, 1989; and Saunders, 1990, for example) have begun to argue that class is no longer a potent force in British social life. Before drawing what ought to have seemed at the very least a counter-intuitive conclusion given the strong and explicit reassertion of the capitalist social prerogative instanced by Thatcherism, it seems to me that they would have been far better advised to have thought again about the representationalist conception of classes as primarily groups of people (Woodiwiss, 1990a, pt. 4; see also, Gibson-Graham, 1996).

In any event and in the present context, what is far more important than this argument is the fact that Marx's theory is not inherently representationalist and so should not be dismissed as an anachronism. If one wanted to select an artistic analogy that summarises Marx's achievement as regards disturbing the 'given array of visual facts', the obvious contrast would be that between John Constable and J.M.W. Turner in his 'all that is solid melts into air' paintings (Http://www.artcyclopedia.com – 'Picture Search', J.M.W. Turner, *Rain, Steam and Speed*).

REPRESENTATIONALISM AND ITS OTHER IN WEBER

Turning now to Weber, his writings suggest that he was probably even less concerned than Marx with language as such and therefore perhaps even less interested in contemporary Linguistics. This was presumably because Neo-Kantianism rendered any such concern largely otiose since it already provided what linguistics could not. This was a semantics or a method of discerning meanings that took into account people's actions as well as their words through adopting a hermeneutic stance and practising *verstehen* or sympathetic understanding; that is, by recommending that observers place themselves in the position of the other, at least in so far as so doing was relevant to the observers' own values. This said, Weber was aware of the comparative philologists. Indeed, he repeats with approval their low opinion of the Chinese language (Gerth and Mills, 1948, pp. 430ff). On the other hand, he would no doubt also have been just as leery as Marx of the Romanticist linguistics of von

Humbolt *et al.*, since this had already led to talk of the 'genius of the German language' which would have sounded deeply suspect to him.

As is well-known, Weber was as staunch a believer in observable or representable facts as the antidote to value biases as Marx, albeit as they concerned subjective meanings as much as they concerned 'statistical uniformities'. Indeed in some ways Weber was an even more insistent advocate of the empiricist variant of representationalism than Marx in that he repeatedly abjured all non-empirically grounded conceptualisations. Thus he pointedly and with some pleasure states at the beginning of Chapter 2 of *Economy and Society*, which concerns the 'sociological categories of economic action', that: 'It has proved possible entirely to avoid the controversial concept of "value" '(ibid., p. 63). What is more, Weber's principal criticism of Marx consisted of demonstrating in the *Protestant Ethic and the Spirit of Capitalism* the difficulties that representable facts concerning the religious differences between a number of European countries created for any purely economic explanation for the rise of capitalism in the West.

The *locus classicus* of Weber's representationalism is the following extract from the first chapter of *Economy and Society*:

For . . . other cognitive purposes – for instance, juristic ones – or for practical ends, it may . . . be convenient or even indispensable to treat social collectivities, such as states, associations, business corporations, foundations, as if they were individual persons . . . . But for the subjective interpretation of action in sociological work these collectivities must be treated as *solely* the resultants and modes of organisation of the particular acts of individual persons since these alone can be treated as agents in a course of subjectively understandable action (ibid., p.13).

Here, then, is clear evidence of how a humanist ontology can reinforce an empiricist ocularcentrism even in the presence of an otherwise idealist ontology. But here too is the statement of a rule whose observance was impossible and therefore caused Weber to retreat from representationalism altogether and not simply from its empiricist variant:

> the same historical phenomena may be in one aspect feudal, in another patrimonial, in another bureaucratic, and in still another charismatic. In order to give a precise meaning to these terms, it is necessary for the sociologist to formulate pure ideal types of the corresponding forms of action which in each case involve the highest possible degree of logical integration by virtue of their complete adequacy at the level of meaning. But, precisely because this is true, it is probably seldom if ever that a real phenomenon corresponds exactly to one of these ideally constructed pure types .... *Theoretical differentiation* ... is possible in sociology only in terms of ideal or pure types (ibid., p. 20, emphasis added)

Moreover:

> The theoretical concepts of sociology are ideal types not only from the objective point of view, but also in their application to subjective processes. In the great majority of cases actual action goes on in a state of inarticulate half-consciousness or

actual unconsciousness of its subjective meaning . . . . The ideal type of meaningful action where the meaning is fully conscious and explicit is the marginal case. Every sociological or historical investigation, in applying its analysis to the empirical facts must take this fact into account . . . . [Nevertheless] [h]e may reason as if action actually proceeded on the basis of clearly self-conscious meaning (ibid., p. 22).

In sum:

> An ideal type is formed by the one-sided accentuation of one or more points of view and by the synthesis of a great many diffuse, discrete, more or less present and occasionally absent *concrete individual phenomena*, which are arranged according to those one-sidedly emphasised viewpoints into a unified analytical construct (Weber, 1949, p. 90, emphasis added).

Considering these four passages together, we have a position which argues that, although human beings are the only real or representable social entities, it is impossible to build socio-logical concepts on pictures of what they do and think because it is often difficult to discern exactly what they are doing, and anyway they themselves do not often know what they are doing or thinking let alone why. However, all is not lost thanks to the possibility of sympathetic understanding which allows the sociologist and his or her logical abilities to take the place of the actual actors when it comes to theoretically picturing their actions by constructing ideal types of them. Here again, then, is the same creative tension between the empiricist and rationalist variants of representationalism as was identified in Marx.

As far as I can tell, Weber's major work, *Economy and Society*, contains not one single item of either reported speech or direct quotation from any archive. Instead, its multitude of ideal types are constructed through a combination of his own immensely wide-ranging scholarship and great logical powers. It is this combination that explains how he moved beyond representationalism instead of simply from the empiricist to the rationalist variant. However, in the current context, it is the significance of the logical powers which is critical since in every instance this involved the deployment of an imagined template of an in itself invisible structure – who has ever seen *zweckrationale* action, capitalism, Protestantism, legal-rational domination, or charisma? Of course the texts upon which Weber drew in producing his monumental synthesis included primary, archival materials and secondary commentaries on such materials – *The Protestant Ethic*, for example, is much closer to the data. However, the fact remains that the subjective meanings in relation to which Weber's ideal types were adequate were his own logical creations, as he would have been the first to acknowledge. As such they were at least as much the product of a non-representationalist theoretical practice as of a representationalist one. Indeed, in a striking anticipation of Saussure's significatory conception of language and its inhabitants, Weber refers to his imagined template as a creative 'representation of the idea' (ibid, p. 91) of whatever might be of interest and not simply the representation of a pre-existing meaning. Moreover, in one of his rare, passing comments on contemporary philology he comes even closer to Saussure and his decision to focus on *langue* rather than *parole* with the following critical comment:

When ... a leading contemporary philologist declares that the subject-matter of philology is the 'speech of *every individual*', even the formulation of such a program is possible only after there is a relatively clear ideal type of the written language, which the otherwise orientationless and unbounded investigation of the infinite variety of speech can utilize (at least tacitly) (Weber, 1949, p. 104, emphasis in the original).

All that said, Weber's explicit commitment to humanism and representationalism in its empiricist form always remained very strong with the result that none of the component elements of any of his ideal types refers to anything that is in principle invisible – all are 'concrete individual phenomena' (ibid, p. 91). Even power is defined in a representationalist way as the 'the chance of a man or a number of men to realize their own will in a communal action even against the resistance of others' (Gerth and Mills, 1948, p. 180). This, it seems to me, explains two things. First, why his sociology contains no conception of social structure as anything other than a very loosely integrated combination of elements which changes according to who is looking at it – Parsons (1937, p. 607) refers to it as 'mosaical', but perhaps kaleidoscopic would be an even better description. Thus Weber's theoretical edifice has none of the elegance of Marx's, or indeed, as we will see, Durkheim's, since all of his concepts refer to the same level of social-structural being in the sense that none pertains to entities or processes that, so to speak, make others possible or encompass them. Even the concept of rationalisation which might

45

appear to pertain to such a process is induced on the basis of the evidence represented in such ideal types as those of 'capitalism', 'Protestantism', 'legal-rational domination', and of course 'bureaucracy'. Lacking an epistemological warrant despite his strong suspicion of ontological depth, Weber's concepts multiplied and spread freely across the surface of the social as in the work of a cartographer concerned to map the world in terms of rainfall, temperature or indeed provinces and nation states. The only limits on their proliferation were Weber's interests and capacity to read.

In sum, then, Weber provided us with a set if not quite a system of conceptual signs rather than representations with the result that they too ought not to be considered anachronistic. Thus many of his concepts, those of the state, domination, bureaucracy and law, for example, have proved to be sufficiently detached from the time and place of their construction – thanks not only to their logically derived structures but also to the comparative scholarship upon which they were based – to be useful, indeed essential, to other scholars, whether Weberian or not, as they have tried to understand very different circumstances and even very different problems. What else, as a further example, is Foucault's (1979) theorisation of power as 'discipline against resistance' but a non-humanist reworking of Weber's definition?

One last comment is necessary, however. And it is that, of course, the rationale for Weber's continuing relevance that has just been provided would not be one that he would have advanced, at least as a first line of defence. Because of his avowed Neo-Kantianism and therefore the role played by 'relevance to value' in selecting problems for sociological investigation from the otherwise impossible complexity of social life, he would have most likely invoked his essay on 'Objectivity' where he argues that there are as many sets of ideal types as there are value positions. As he says 'all knowledge of cultural reality . . . is always knowledge *from particular points of view*' (Weber, 1949, p. 81). Thus, if he were still alive, and although they often fail to acknowledge their filiation, he would point to today's 'feminist standpoint epistemologists' (Harding, 1984) and 'Queer Theorists' (Seidman, 1996) as well as today's, most often British, 'Left-Weberians' (Marshall, 1997), as still applying his method and so assuring its continuing relevance. Finally, if one had to find an artistic analogy to summarise Weber's achievement, the obvious candidate would be the cubist Picasso since during this period he drew attention to the different angles of vision without denying the reality of the scene so surveyed and rearranged.

REPRESENTATIONALISM AND ITS OTHER IN DURKHEIM

Although there is once again little direct evidence in his texts that Durkheim had engaged with the Linguistics of his day any more seriously than Marx or Weber, it seems clear to me at least that he would have been much more sympathetic to the Romanticist linguists and their idea that language could shape thought than either of the other two. Thus, discussing the possible nature of a future 'social psychology', he says:

As for the laws of the collective formation of ideas, these are . . . completely unknown . . . . What should be done is to investigate, by comparing mythical themes, legends and popular traditions, and *languages*, how social representations are attracted to or exclude each other, amalgamate with or are distinguishable from one another (Durkheim, 1982, pp. 41–2, emphasis added).

Prophetically, he refers to the Stoics in Chapter 1 of *The Rules of Sociological Method* of 1895 and uses the term 'a system of signs' to refer to language. Furthermore, in the same place, and developing the ideas about the importance of the 'conscience collective' that he had set out in his first book, *The Division of Labour in Society* of 1893, he insisted that the 'social facts' in which he was interested consisted of 'representations and actions'. Moreover, he made it clear that it was the representations that took linguistic form that were the most important objects of sociological interest. Indeed it was this form that allowed representations to be considered as social facts at all in that this made them external to individuals in his double sense of being both constraining and visible.

In this last point, however, there is also evidence of Durkheim's commitment to the empiricist variant of representationalism; that is, his insistence alongside Marx and Weber that social science should start from the visible or the picturable. This, then, gives us one meaning of his first rule of sociological method: 'consider social facts as things' (Durkheim 1982, p. 60). I will discuss the second and ultimately predominant meaning below after I have outlined the developing tension between the empiricist and rationalist forms of representationalism within his thought. The first meaning is reinforced by the rule's first corollary: 'one must systematically discard all pre-conceptions' (ibid., p. 72). However, the rules that follow all qualify this first rule in one way or another. And the result is that Durkheim's eventual definition of sociology's object of study is not so much the product of observation or a representationalist practice as of a very particular and highly abstract, non-representationalist visuality.

One can clearly see this movement beginning and developing in his presentation of the otherwise insistently representationalist second rule and some of his comments on it:

> [The second rule is that] the subject matter of research must only include a group of phenomena defined beforehand by certain common external characteristics and all phenomena which correspond to this definition must be so included . . . . When research is only just beginning and the facts have not yet been submitted to any analysis, their sole ascertainable characteristics are those sufficiently external to be immediately apparent. Those less apparent are doubtless more essential. Their explanatory value is greater, but they remain unknown at this stage of scientific knowledge and cannot be visualised save by substituting for reality some conception of the mind (ibid., p. 75).

It is certainly not true that the commonly held concept is useless to the scientist. It serves as a benchmark, indicating to him that somewhere there exists a cluster of phenomena bearing the same name and which consequently are likely to possess common characteristics (ibid., p. 76).

But, it will be claimed, to define phenomena by their visible characteristics, is this not to attribute to superficial properties

a kind of preponderance over more fundamental qualities?
. . . But the reproach is based upon a confusion. Since the
definition . . . is made at the beginnings of the science its
purpose could not be to express the essence of reality; rather
it is intended to equip us to arrive at this essence later. Its
sole function is to establish contact with things, and since
these cannot be reached by the mind save from the outside, it
is by externalities that it expresses them (ibid., p. 80).

Several things strike me as remarkable about these passages and
the movement between the rule and its first two corollaries.
The first is how aware of the difference between vision and
visuality Durkheim is, although, of course, he does not use
these terms. The second is how clear he is about the ultimate
explanatory superiority of an abstract visuality over one that is
merely vision-based. The third is that even in the earliest stages
of a science there is a place for 'commonly held concepts'. The
fourth is that, in nevertheless maintaining a privileged place for
vision-based concepts, he is talking about the foundation of a
science not about the start of any research project, as is
commonly supposed by those who read him as an empiricist.
The fifth is that what one can hear in these passages is, quite
literally, one of Foucault's authorities of delimitation preparing
to present his template for the discipline (see below, p. 149).

Indeed the need for such a template is announced just two
pages after the last of the passages quoted above:

An observation is more objective the more stable the object
is to which it relates . . . . If the sole reference points given
are themselves variable . . . no common measure at all exists

... so long as social life has not succeeded in isolating itself from the particular events which embody it, in order that it may constitute itself as a separate entity, it is precisely this difficulty that remains .... Thus social life consists of free-ranging forces ... which the observer's scrutinising gaze does not succeed in fixing mentally. The consequence is that this approach is not open to the scientist embarking on the study of social reality .... Apart from the individual acts to which they give rise, collective habits are expressed in definite forms such as legal or moral rules, popular sayings, or facts of social structure, etc. As these forms exist permanently and do not change... they constitute a fixed object, a constant standard which is always at hand for the observer, and which leaves no room for subjective impressions (ibid., p. 82).

Thus the third corollary of the second rule is as follows: '[W]hen the sociologist undertakes to investigate any order of social facts he must strive to consider them from a viewpoint where they present themselves in isolation from their individual manifestations' (ibid. p. 83). In other words, a chapter that begins with a rule that ostensibly stresses the primacy of vision ends with a clear statement of the scientific unavoidability of a specific and abstractly defined visuality for sociology. And, moreover, so far from being an instance of self-contradiction, this movement is achieved through self-clarification.

In the remainder of the *Rules* Durkheim continues to develop his non-representationalist conception of sociological method and indeed of the social. Thus he argues in Chapter 4 that observation is not only pointless without classification but also that classification requires the selection of '*decisive* or *crucial* facts' (ibid., p. 110, emphasis in the original) which become clear 'without plunging too deeply into the study of the facts' (Ibid., p. 111). Indeed, he goes on to suggest that the basic principle of selection is already known:

> Once . . . [the] notion of the horde or single-segment society has been assumed – whether it is conceived of as a historical reality or as a *scientific postulate* – we possess the necessary support on which to construct the complete scale of social types (ibid., pp. 113–14, emphasis added).

Now one does not have to agree with what Paul Hirst (1975) has termed Durkheim's 'elementarianism' to be able to appreciate the fact that in this passage Durkheim is perfectly properly, in terms of realist criteria at least, acknowledging the necessarily theory-laden nature of observation. Nor should it make any difference that his source of inspiration was Herbert Spencer.

In Chapter 5 he argues for and explicitly declares sociality to be a *sui generis* phenomenon: 'society is not the mere sum of individuals, but the system formed by their association represents a specific reality which has its own characteristics' (ibid., p. 129). This gives the second meaning to the term 'social fact', and in the remainder of the chapter Durkheim specifies its consequences for causal analysis:

> Collective representations, emotions and tendencies have not as their causes certain states of consciousness of individuals, but the conditions under which the body social as a whole exists (ibid., p. 131).

The determining cause of a social fact must be sought among antecedent social facts and not among the states of the individual consciousness (ibid., p. 134).

The net epistemological effect of this is that his commitment to empiricist representationalism becomes still more tenuous since the 'union of elements' that is the social 'constitutes an inner environment' (ibid., p. 135) that is therefore invisible. The chapter concludes with confirmation of this in a striking anticipation of Foucault's argument in *Discipline and Punish* (1977):

The rules we have set out would . . . allow a sociology to be constructed which would see in *the spirit of discipline*, the essential condition for all common life, while at the same time founding it on reason and truth (ibid., p. 144, emphasis added).

Chapter 6, the final chapter, makes an argument for the centrality of the comparative method in Sociology whose particularity and rigour are still too little appreciated. Not only is comparative work 'sociology itself, in so far as it ceases to be purely descriptive' (ibid., p. 157), but also it is not simply a matter of comparing randomly chosen instances of whatever is of interest:

[They must be part of a] series of variations, systematically constituted, whose terms are correlated with each other in as continuous a gradation as possible and which moreover cover an adequate range (ibid., p. 155; for my own illustrative attempt to abide by this rule, see Woodiwiss, 1998).

Another anticipation of Foucault occurs in the course of making this argument when Durkheim makes the following comment on data:

> Since they do not require to be numerous, the documents can be selected, and what is more, studied closely . . . . Therefore . . . [the sociologist] can, and consequently must, take as the chief material of his inductions societies whose beliefs, traditions, customs and law have been embodied in written and authentic records. Undoubtedly he will not disdain the information supplied by the ethnographer [or social survey, A.W.]. (No facts can be disdained by the scientist.) But he will assign them to their appropriate place. Instead of making them the nub of his researches, he will generally use them only to supplement those which he gleans from history, or at the very least he will try to confirm them by the latter (ibid., pp. 153–4).

In other words, Durkheim both suggests that discourse analysis should be the principal mode of analysis in sociology and explains why – it is less likely to be the artefact of the observer's understandings than either ethnographic or survey data. As I learnt many years ago from my methods teacher and later a colleague at Essex, Tony Coxon, the latter are more accurately described as *capta*.

In sum, Durkheim's representationalism was subverted almost from the very beginning by the strength of his conviction as to sociality's undepictable *sui generis* character. Hence his belief in the possibility of classification, the existence of internal causal processes and the necessity of the comparative method.

54

Hence his substantive concepts which in every case are in themselves both invisible and deductions made possible by sociality's *sui generis* character: for example, 'the division of labour', 'the conscience collective', 'anomie' and 'suicidogenic currents'. Hence in particular the remarkable substantive conception of 'collective representations' that he eventually provided in *The Elementary Forms of the Religious Life*:

> [C]ollective consciousness is something more than a mere epiphenomenon of its morphological basis . . . . In order that the former may appear, a synthesis *sui generis* of particular consciousnesses is required. Now this synthesis has the effect of disengaging a whole world of sentiments, ideas and images which, once born, obey laws of their own. They attract each other, repel each other, unite, divide themselves, and multiply, though these combinations are not commanded and necessitated by the condition of the underlying reality. The life thus brought into being even enjoys so great an independence that it sometimes indulges in manifestations with no purpose or utility of any sort, for the pleasure of affirming itself (Durkheim, 1976, pp. 423–4).

Hence, finally, his summary and strikingly three-dimensional biological metaphor of society as a morphological entity (to be studied as the social ecology of human populations) with an *interior* physiological structure (to be studied as the various institutional sociologies of religion, law, etc.) (Traugott, 1978, pp. 71–90). Although Durkheim uses the term 'substratum' when referring to morphology, this does not mean that he has simply recast Marx's architectural metaphor since the relations it suggests are those of interior/exterior rather than base/

superstructure. Likewise, although he uses the term 'functions' when referring to the internal structure of the social, this does not mean that he was a functionalist since for him, contrary to what a functionalist would argue, the 'utility of a [social] fact is not what causes its existence, [although] it must generally be useful to continue to survive' (Durkheim, 1982, p. 124). Sadly, and mainly because of such misreadings, we have neglected for too long what in my view is sociology's best insight into what social structure might look like and how its relations to its human embodiments might be most usefully conceived.

Finally, if one wished to find an artistic analogy to summarise Durkheim's achievements, I would suggest the work of Escher since for the two of them the world is highly structured in a three-dimensional form that is as yet both largely unknown and unlikely to correspond to our common-sense conceptions of what that structuring might look like.

CONCLUSION

In sum, the answer to my question 'Are the concepts of the classical theorists inherently representationalist?' must be 'No'. In each case they transcended the limitations of the Linguistics and indeed idealist and empiricist philosophical prejudices of their day because of the exigencies of practical social scientific work. That is, it was precisely because each of them was fiercely committed to substantive research that they pushed empiricist representationalism to its limits, found it wanting and, largely unknowingly, transcended it. As Marx (1867, p. 8) put the point about the necessity of substantive research:

The physicist either observes physical phenomena where they occur in their most typical form and most free from disturbing influence, or, wherever possible, he makes experiments under conditions that assure the occurrence of the phenomenon in its normality. In this work I have to examine the capitalist mode of production and the conditions of production and exchange corresponding to that mode. Up to the present time their classic ground is England. That is the reason why England is used as the chief illustration of the development of my theoretical ideas.

In the absence of such a research context and as will be demonstrated in the following chapter, the almost inevitable result is rationalistic representationalism. It is therefore important to enunciate a first rule of neo-classical method:

it is a necessary but not a sufficient condition of non-representationalist theoretical development that it is undertaken in the context of substantive research.

In terms of their contribution at the level of the discursive formation that makes any sociological discourse possible and by the same token disqualifies any discourse that is not so constrained, the legacy of the founding trio comprises at least the following:

1 a shared convergence with respect to the unavoidability of an ordinary realist metatheoretical foundation for sociological work because this is what is required by the transcendence of representationalism. This is a well-established

reading of Marx and Durkheim (Benton, 1977; Keat and Urry, 1975) but suggests a new one of Weber

2 a shared conception of the social as a distinct realm of nature which only Durkheim made explicit but the other two acknowledged implicitly through their submission to what realist epistemology regards as the logical necessity of an abstract moment pertaining to an initially invisible element or process in the production of sociological representations

3 an emergent conception of the nature of this distinct realm (that is, of social structure) in Weber's intuition that there is something that was indescribable about the social, Marx's attempt to conceptualise this something with his metaphor of base and superstructure, and Durkheim's better double metaphor of morphology and physiology wherein the latter is the interior of the former

4 shared agreement that the principal dimensions of sociality are the economic, the political, the cultural and the even more complex forms of life they make possible either by themselves or, most often and as in the case of class, through their imbrication with one another

5 a plurality of insights and conceptualisations concerning the specific nature of these forms of life and their inter-relationships with one another − the capitalist mode of production, bureaucracy and collective representations, for example − which should be synthesisable or at least translatable into each others' terms once they have been cleansed, so to speak, of any representationalist residue whatever its local content or metatheoretical cause − rationalism, humanism or empiricism for example

Thus the reason why their texts became and remain constitutive of social theory was and is not simply because of the past and present pertinence of the problems they addressed (see below, pp. 158–61) but also because their concepts have proved or could yet prove to be reworkable in the context of changing circumstances since they were not indelibly marked by a specific representationalist content. Of course they focused on particular problems and issues but this does not necessarily exclude other problems from, and foci for, sociological analysis. Indeed, to invert what my Essex colleague Miriam Glucksman has recently been arguing in an excellent lecture to final year students, one may argue that the sociology of gender, for example, would be literally unthinkable without the contributions of the classical authors.

For Glucksman and to paraphrase drastically, with their concepts of class, the division of labour and status, the classical theorists only got so far in providing us with the means to think the sociology of gender – women are a subordinate group, occupying specific positions in the division of labour, and deprived of social honour. But by the same token, one may equally well argue that the classical concepts were what made it possible to think about gender at all in a sociological way. This point is reinforced once one considers the use that the early theorists of 'race' as a social category, such as W.E.B. Dubois and Oliver Cromwell Cox, made of Marx and Weber's ideas in developing their own.

Some at least amongst subsequent generations of theorists consider the classical theorists to be the founders and definers of the discipline, but what have we made of their legacy? Regrettably, or so I will argue in the following two chapters, the answer must be 'not enough', and this is because so few of the better-known theorists have maintained the classical author's non-representationalist understanding of the nature of concepts and, therefore, theory. Indeed, tragically, many individuals among the subsequent generations of sociologists appear to have been so impressed by the power of the founders' concepts that they took them as accurate, or allegedly accurate, pictures of social reality that could be either refined, rejected or taken as authorising their own, very differently produced efforts. Thus, there has been disappointingly little work on either extending the founders' work by applying and, if necessary, reworking it and so filling in the numerous gaps in their theoretical systems or translating their concepts into each others' terms. Instead, we have seen what I have termed elsewhere (Woodiwiss, 1990a, p. 9) a 'rush to representation' of a very peculiar kind – representation without investigation, without research, without even looking at any social things, in a phrase 'hyper-rationalist representationalism'. Thus, on the part of both the supporters and detractors of the classics, theorising has tended to become palimpsestic, a matter of commenting upon and restating rather than reworking theoretical texts in the course of substantive, explanatory investigations. The result is that in some instances, notable amongst the supporters of the classics would be the work of Talcott Parsons and Anthony Giddens, conceptual nets have been flung over almost the whole of social life that are even broader than Weber's but lack the strength provided by the warp of his substantive researches, the weft of his metatheoretical consistency and the interweaving of the two consequent upon his explanatory purpose. The tragedy lies in the fact that in both cases this was the result of what turned out to be a deadly combination of the overestimation of the ill-understood achievements of the founders and the desire to see them turned to good, substantive analytical effect.

CHAPTER TWO

The Regression to Vision in Contemporary Social Theory

> What is that fear which makes you reply in terms
> of consciousness when someone talks to you about
> a practice, its conditions, its rules and its historical
> transformations? What is that fear which makes
> you seek, beyond all boundaries, ruptures, shifts
> and divisions, the great historico-transcendental
> destiny of the Occident?
>
> Michel Foucault (1972, pp. 209–10)

When one looks at contemporary social theory through the prism of the vision/visuality opposition, and if one considers the latter to be an advance over the former, something happens that is pleasingly surprising in that it reminds one of looking through a corrected *camera obscura* such as that in Edinburgh's Outlook Tower – the world is confirmed to be as one has always imagined it. Specifically, that which has often been dismissively referred to as the 'mainstream' may be seen as the avant-garde, and much of the so-called avant-garde may be seen as a regression.

This chapter looks at what some contemporary social theorists have done with the classical legacy in order to assess the progress or otherwise of what I am proposing as the non-representationalist, neo-classical project. The discussion that follows focuses on British texts. This is partly because of their current global prominence but also because of the particular nature of British social theory. Not since Herbert Spencer and not until Anthony Giddens's recent work has Britain produced a novel and overarching social theory of the kind produced in both Continental Europe and the United States. There are many possible reasons for this – the lack of a full-blown bourgeois revolution and the consequent grip of empiricism on our national culture (Anderson, 1992), the closeness of the early British sociologists to the policy-making establishment (Abrams, 1968), the absence of talent, or all of these (Turner, 1994, Ch. 11). In any event, the British forte, if that is what it is, has been to look critically at the theoretical systems that others have produced and devise ways in which those ideas which pass our very various tests – most importantly practical explanatory utility – might be synthesised with one another. The result is that the British mainstream has been neither especially hostile to theory, as is the case with much American sociology, nor over-excited by it. In other words, British social theory provides a particularly promising field of investigation for one interested in finding signs of an emerging neo-classicism, since it has been especially concerned with the practical representational power of theory. By the same token, the fact that I will be able to point to few such signs in this and the following chapter is, frankly, irritating as well as somewhat dispiriting. Over the next two chapters I will have some hard things to say about some of the texts I will consider. This is certainly not because they are the worst ones around nor indeed is my irritation directed at their authors. On the contrary, the texts I will consider are amongst the very best and it is the rest of us who should be blamed if some of their authors have been allowed to get away with what is almost literally sociological murder. Finally, in so far as I intend that my selection should be representative of a good proportion of contemporary macro-theory, it is so relative only to my purpose of assessing the progress or otherwise of a putative, non-representationalist, neo-classical project.

THE PECULIARITIES OF THE BRITISH

I will begin with what to me at least is the good news and say a little bit more about why I think that the British sociological temperament might be thought to be especially supportive of any neo-classical project. I will make my point by offering a few comments concerning Marshall's seminal essay 'Citizenship and social class', since not only was it published in 1949, and therefore at the beginning of what in terms of British sociology is the contemporary period, but it was also written by one of its then undoubted authorities of delimitation. Marshall's essay wears its theory very lightly indeed – 'class' is in the title and 'status' in the text, but there are no theoretical references at all in the notes. Instead most of the text and all of the notes relate to British history over the preceding two or three hundred years. Nevertheless, so profound was Marshall's grasp of the concepts he deployed that they not only transformed our way of looking at what was already a well-worked period of our history, but their use also produced, for the first time, a sociological concept of citizenship because of the way in which he articulated 'class' and 'status' in relation to the data at his disposal. Here, then, very early on, was a striking demonstration of the potential power of an approach that I would term neo-classical: first, concepts from Marx and Weber were combined in recognition of their necessary, if in this case unexplained, complimentarity; and second, 'class' and 'status' were clearly understood not as pictures of what existed but in their non-representationalist senses as means of looking – their articulation with one another would not have been possible otherwise and could not have produced the further necessity of 'citizenship'. In sum, Marshall's neo-classicism turned an account of British social history into a text which has gained global significance – *vide*, not only the present omnipresence of his sense of the term 'citizenship' in academic and public debate (Turner, 1986; Turner and Hamilton, 1994), but also the essential nature of his categories of 'civil', 'political' and 'social' rights to contemporary global discussions of human rights.

THE INTERNATIONALISATION OF BRITISH SOCIAL THEORY

Two events above all made it very difficult for British sociologists wishing to make a theoretical contribution ever again to wear their theory as lightly as Marshall had done. These were the delayed reception of Parsonian theory in the late 1950s and the even more delayed reception of continental European Marxism in the 1960s. Neither of these events in themselves need have caused problems for the emergence of a robust, non-representationalist social theory, particularly since they occurred so close together and therefore produced a conflict whose most obvious mode of resolution would have been through the court of substantive research, or should have been. Despite the early, Weber-inspired, empiricist representationalism apparent in his concept of the 'unit act' and the general 'analytical realism' of the reading of the classical authors set out in *The Structure of Social Action*, Parsons took up a much more obviously Durkheim-inspired, non-representationalist stance in his later work and with considerable gusto – or so one might think. The most influential statement of this new position was *The Social System* (1951). The problems with any claim that might be made that the new position was non-representationalist, are twofold. First, in deference to his earlier representationalism Parsons conceived of the social as an emergent property of individual interactions. This limited, still in a Weberian fashion, what he could allow himself to theorise – only things that were observable. Second and in contrast to Weber, he compounded this problem by violating what I have called the first rule of neo-classical method, by not developing his theory in the context of an ongoing programme of substantive research. Thus, in a rationalistic representationalist mode, he created an apparently complex model of the social which was not so much at one or two removes from its referent but, rather, markedly to its side.

Untested against the actual recalcitrance of the social, his concepts were only as effective a mode of seeing as his initial imaginative effort could make them. Inevitably, that first effort was wanting, whether because of the absence of Marx's concepts of the capitalist economy, Weber's comparative scholarship, or whatever. The result was that his concepts were for the most part purely imagined pictures of social reality possessing none of the substantive and universalistic purchase of Weber's. Indeed one of his core concepts, a crude version of Durkheim's *conscience collective* which he termed the 'central value system', comprised a big picture – in cinemascope even – of what the social relations in the pertinent society supposedly looked like: in terms of his 'pattern-variable schema', they were either affective or affectively neutral, collectivistic or individualistic, particularistic or universalistic, ascription or achievement-orientated, and finally diffuse or specific in their scope. What is as striking now as the formalism of these terms, which latter quality many have commented upon, is their representationalism; in other words, each of them singles out a potentially observable aspect or pattern of behaviour. The consequence is that, although Parsons' conception of social structure has a three-dimensional form which is now its most admired feature, the space so demarcated is almost empty. This is not surprising, given that its parameters are a purely imagined picture of social structure and a potential means of grounding this picture which is restricted to its observable parts only. There is therefore an incommensurability between these parameters which means that even if the unobserved had been observed the results could not have enriched the concept of social structure.

At the heart of Parsons's concept of social structure and therefore of his attempt to specify the *sui generis* character of the social are his AGIL model and the category of 'status-role'. The AGIL model specifies (admittedly provisionally) the four universal functional problems and therefore the core social institutions as: Adaptation to the external environment (the occupational structure), Goal-attainment (the polity); Integration (the legal system); and Latency (the family). 'Status-role' is a combinatory concept created by combining 'status', which refers to a position in an institution, with 'role' which refers to the performance in such a position. Both of these sound as suspiciously like a common-sense conception of social structure to me, as they did to Mills (1959) so many years ago – social structure is the different things people do and how they do them. The ultimately commonsensical nature of Parsons's insights is confirmed when one considers the 'fundamental theorem of sociology' (Parsons, 1951, p. 42) or Parsons's suggestion that what gives society its coherence is the 'reciprocity of role expectations' that the socialisation of actors into the ruling set of pattern-variable choices ensures – people generally know what to expect of each other thanks to how they were brought up. All this said, and for ill rather than for good, the Parsons who has been most influential in British sociology has been the Parsons of *The Structure of Social Action*, which I think can fairly be said to have mesmerised many British sociologists, up to and including Giddens, as the best social theory we never had.

On the topic of continental European Marxist theory, my comments will be even more condensed. This is because I have written extensively on its importance as a contribution to a possible non-representationalist sociology elsewhere (Woodiwiss, 1990a). All I will say here is that several factors explain why its contribution has been far greater than that of Parsonian theory. First, as a development of a theory that was already well-grounded and contested in substantive research, rather than a completely new theory, even its new or reworked conceptualisations immediately gained a resonance, a thickness if you like. Only a massive new research programme could have obtained such a resonance for the Parsonian concepts, and then only if one discounts the incommensurability problem identified above. Thus even the work of the determinedly abstract Louis Althusser was read substantively; that is, for the new sense that it either did or did not make of existing modellings of social structure (Hindess and Hirst, 1975). Second, Althusser was by no means as dominant a figure in relation to his field of endeavour as Parsons was in relation to his. Several of what one might call Althusser's competitors were committed to theoretical agendas that were at least as powerfully innovative as his, notably the Neo-Gramscians such as Ernesto Laclau and the Critical Theorists whose dominant figure was and remains Habermas. Thus Althusser's innovations were not only a product of critical reflection on existing practice but also entered a complex theoretical and substantive domain wherein they were tested, almost to destruction. One result was that many of the insights of Durkheim and Weber were thereby incorporated into Marxist theory although regrettably their provenance was seldom acknowledged. Another is that it is inconceivable that there could ever be an Althusserian revival like that recently attempted on Parsons's behalf – Althusser made a very significant difference to Marxist theory but he did not entirely recast it in the manner that Parsons attempted in relation to social theory more generally.

LOCKWOOD AND NON-REPRESENTATIONALIST SOCIAL THEORY

Perhaps the most sustained and creative, non-marxist, British response to all of this theoretical ferment has been the work of

Lockwood, who was a student of Marshall's at the London School of Economics. One way, although not necessarily his own, of describing Lockwood's theoretical achievement is to say that, in responding to functionalist theory in particular, he initiated the self-conscious pursuit of the neo-classical project by making Marshall's dialogue between Marxist and Weberian theory explicit, bringing Durkheim into the conversation, and as a result greatly deepening our understanding of the nature and wider social significance of the status order as a complex structural nexus. However, Lockwood's non-representation-alism is part of the package he inherited rather than the result of a conscious process of metatheoretical ratiocination. Indeed, consciously, Lockwood is one of those who believes in the promise of *The Structure of Social Action,* but with a huge saving grace that I will identify shortly.

After delivering some acute criticisms of Parson's *Social System* and writing a major work of historical sociology, *The Blackcoated Worker* (1958), Lockwood's first significant theoretical statement was his article 'Social integration and system integration' (1964). Somewhat surprisingly, given that it was written by someone who was already well-known for the acuity of his Weber-inspired criticisms, this article is a defence of what Lockwood calls 'general functionalism' (that is, functionalism without the Parsonian stress on the stability that follows from value consensus) against the criticisms of such 'conflict theorists' as John Rex (1961) and Ralf Dahrendorf (1959). The basis for this defence is provided by the 'wholly artificial' (that is, purely analytical or observationally unjustifiable) distinction between the two different sorts of problems that societies face; namely, those of 'social integration' which refers to the 'orderly or conflictual relationships between the *actors'* in a social system, and 'system integration' which refers to the 'orderly or conflictual relationships between the *parts'* of a social system (Lockwood, 1964, p. 400). On my reading, the former refers to the visible and the latter to the invisible aspects of social relations. In any event, the point that Lockwood makes with this distinction is that, while the conflict theorists quite properly criticise the normative functionalists for their consensual account of social integration, they neglect the significance of the general functionalist insight as to the importance of system integration which, to repeat, could be either orderly or conflictual. What made this neglect surprising to Lockwood was the fact that both of the major sources of inspiration for the conflict theorists, Marx and Weber, developed approaches which not only implicitly acknowledged the difference between the two different modes of integration but related them to one another. Thus Marx argues that system contradictions lead to class conflict, and Weber argues more specifically that, for example, a centralised patrimonial bureaucracy's need for tax revenue leads to the unintentional empowering of the local lords who gather the taxes and who may then challenge the centre. The article ends with this summary of Lockwood's position:

1 The propensity to social change arising from the functional incompatibility between an institutional order and its material base has been ignored by normative functionalists because of their concentration on the moral aspects of social integration.
2 It has been equally ignored by conflict theorists, who, in concentrating on the weakness of the normative function-

alist approach to social integration, have failed to relate their interest in social change to the problem of system integration (ibid., p. 412)

Read in the light of what precedes it, this summary makes it clear that for Lockwood an adequate social theory has not only to attend to both sets of problems but also that the classical theorists provide a better guide than either set of newer theorists. This is why I regard him as a neo-classicist.

After completing another highly influential piece of theoretically informed, substantive sociological research, the co-authored *Affluent Worker* studies (Goldthorpe *et al.*, 1969), Lockwood returned to theoretical questions. The overall results of his prolonged rumination on them finally saw the light of day with the publication of his book *Solidarity and Schism: 'The Problem of Disorder' in Durkheimian and Marxist Sociology* (1992). Lockwood begins his argument in what to me is an unpromising manner by saying that he intends that his contribution should be 'at the level of social rather than system integration'; that is, at the level of the visible rather than the invisible aspects of social relations. However, so far from introducing a slew of new, representationalist concepts, what these comments introduce instead is a profound deepening of our appreciation of the three-dimensional character of social structure. This is because he in fact follows his own guidelines for an adequate social theory as set out at the end of his 1964 article. Not only does he spend most of the book thinking through the nature of some important aspects of system integration, but he clearly suggests that these contain the key to understanding the related aspects of social integration.

Lockwood's focus concerns what Parsons referred to as 'the problem of order' but reconfigured as 'the problem of disorder' to take account of the Marxist insights that Parsons excluded. In other words, the book seeks to understand how it is that societies can accommodate and indeed institutionalise high degrees of conflict without either descending into chaos or undergoing revolutionary change. Essentially, he finds the answer to this question, like Marshall, in the status order. Not only in the development of citizenship but more particularly in the latter's articulation with the stratification system. Status is, of course, a Weberian concept, but Lockwood also finds it to be a necessary and indeed latent concept within the Marxist and Durkheimian accounts of social order and disorder. How Lockwood does this is what is especially interesting in the present context. This is because it provides a paradigm case of the theoretical craft required for neo-classical reasoning: the translating into or, better, the finding in the theoretical structures of one tradition the concepts of the others. My account will do scant justice to the subtlety and scholarship of the original but I hope it serves its purpose nonetheless.

Lockwood's strategy in relation to Durkheim is a two-stage one. First, he thinks through the latter's explanation for social solidarity and fills in the gaps. Durkheim himself points to ritual or hyper-ritual as the means by which what is to Lockwood the essentially moral condition of social solidarity is maintained or renewed. However, Lockwood points out that, as a residual aspect of Durkheim's own reasoning, what makes ritual/hyper-ritual necessary are disturbances that have their sources outside the moral order. Lockwood therefore concludes that what must generally underpin solidarity is an acceptance of a particular hierarchical ordering of the bundle of economic, social and political positions that Weber termed status and Durkheim himself referred to, in a sense close to Marx's, as 'social classification'. Taking his cue from a footnote in Durkheim's *Suicide*, and drawing heavily on Weber's studies of the religions of India and China to fill out its meaning, Lockwood terms this acceptance 'conditional fatalism' (see also, the discussion in Pearce, 1989, pp. 122–3).

The second stage of Lockwood's strategy is to think through Durkheim's explanation of *anomie*, which he takes as Durkheim's antithesis to solidarity. Again he points out that Durkheim explains the onset of an anomic condition as the result of sudden changes in spheres of social life that are external to that of morality, such as the economy. Thus *anomie* is a result of 'de-classification' or a breakdown of the status order. However, such a breakdown seldom results in anything like the outbreak of a war of all against all that, on Lockwood's reading, Durkheim seems to imagine it should. On the contrary, it appears to Lockwood that any such destabilisation of the status order more often than not frees at least one or more segments of the population from the embrace of fatalism, allowing them to attempt to restructure the status system to their advantage. Either as part of such a restructuring effort or definitely after one has been successfully achieved, the newly advantaged group most often engages in efforts at 'moral innovation' which it seeks to embed through the establishment of new rituals. In sum, by approaching Durkheim's problem of order/disorder from both ends, so to speak, and joining up their respective chains of reasoning, Lockwood not only finds the concepts status and class necessary to Durkheim's reasoning but latent within it.

My account of how Lockwood finds 'status' in Marx's work can be even briefer. This is because the argument is far less innovative than that with respect to Durkheim and largely consists of reading developments that had already occurred within the Marxist tradition in a particular way. Lockwood's discussion of Marxism opens by contrasting the well worked out nature of its understanding of the sources of economic contradictions with its very underdeveloped understanding of class consciousness; that is, he contrasts its understanding of the complexity of at least one aspect of system integration with its underdeveloped understanding of what is to him a critical element of social integration. The discussion then moves on to consider and find unconvincing the traditional Marxist explanation for the failure of systemic contradictions to eventuate in revolutions – weaknesses in political leadership. In Lockwood's view, improvements in citizenship rights and therefore the enhanced status of the proletariat provide a far better explanation. He takes this point to have been more and more freely acknowledged by Marxists themselves as they have adopted and developed Gramsci's concept of hegemony.

Disappointingly, instead of showing either how a concept of the status order is a necessary complement to that of hegemony or vice versa, Lockwood ends by berating Marxists for not investigating the internal differentiation of the working class – the topic of his own substantive researches – but instead spending so much time on trying to understand the growth and significance of the middle classes. This is additionally disappointing because, in my view, not only are the latter two topics closely related to one another but also what Marxists have tried to do in the literature on the middle classes is precisely to acknowledge lessons learnt from, if not accredited to, Weber and Durkheim, concerning the omnipresence of the political and discursive dimensions in social life (Woodiwiss, 1990a). Added to these disappointments, should be four disagreements, all of which are related to one another. The first concerns Lockwood's very Parsonian reading of Durkheim's concept of solidarity as basically a moral or cultural phenomenon. The second concerns his neglect of Durkheim's stress on the necessity for a decline in the significance of the conscience collective if the division of labour is to develop beyond a rudimentary level and with solidaristic effects. The third concerns his neglect of Durkheim's concepts of the 'anomic' and 'forced' forms of the division of labour. And the fourth concerns his choice of *Suicide* over *The Division of Labour* as his source for understanding what Durkheim meant by *anomie*. However, were he to adopt my readings, it would simply make it easier for Lockwood to make his point about Durkheim's repressed theory of class.

Notwithstanding my disappointments and our disagreements, it is very clear to me that Lockwood has made a huge contribution to our understanding of the complexity and density of at least a certain region of the social structure, namely that interaction between economic, cultural and political relations that produces the status system. More specifically, and to repeat, although he states that he intends his contribution to be to the understanding of social integration, which it may well be if I allowed myself to think about such things, Lockwood makes his points by arguing almost exclusively at the level of system integration and therefore at the level of the undepictable. In so doing his work demonstrates both the possibility and the potential of theorising in a non-representationalist, neo-classical manner and therefore in terms of an articulated set of signs that have gained their purchase on and therefore their capacity to illuminate the social by their refinement in the process of substantive research.

There is no sign in Lockwood's work of any engagement with post-structuralism, let alone with Foucault; that is, with those who have done most to formalise the non-representationalist mode of theorising. This may well prove to have been a blessing in disguise so far as any possible neo-classicism is concerned. I say this because several equally influential British theorists have engaged with post-structuralism and in my view have come badly unstuck whether the terms of their engagement were negative or positive.

GIDDENS AND THE REGRESSION TO VISION

Giddens's engagement with post-structuralism has been almost entirely negative since he appears to have accepted the accuracy of idealist readings of it (see below, pp. 155–7) and decided to have nothing to do with it (Giddens, 1984, p. 32). However, in this case the results were not benign so far as the prospects for a neo-classical social theory are concerned. This is because the alternate theory of language that he takes up is that of the later Wittgenstein which is a variant of the representation- alist paradigm. Thus the results are in fact broadly the same as would have been the case had he taken up the idealist reading of post-structuralism. What distinguishes the Wittgensteinian variant of representationalism is its insistence that words gain meaning through their collective human use in an ever-changing world rather than as a result of a simple picturing. After some twenty years as an avid reader of, and writer about, classical and an extraordinarily wide selection of contemporary social theory, Giddens decided to make his own effort to transcend the 'babble of rival theoretical voices' (ibid., p. xvi). The result was *The Constitution of Society*. The book and its presentation of 'structuration theory' is undoubtedly a *tour de force* in the way in which it defines a distinctive, new starting point for social theory and the facility with which it spins off new or transformed senses of older conceptionalisations. Unfortunately, it is also a *tour de représentation* and therefore, in my terms, a *tour de régression*.

How does this happen? The key to answering this question lies in noting what Giddens, influenced by his Wittgensteinian reading of the nature of the 'linguistic turn' in philosophy, identifies as 'certain common themes' in the current theoretical confusion and which he in turn uses to define his starting point. These themes are:

1 an emphasis on the 'active, reflexive character of human conduct'
2 the according of a 'fundamental role to language and to cognitive faculties in the explanation of social life'
3 'the declining importance of empiricist philosophies of natural science . . . [which means] that a philosophy of natural science must take account of just those social phenomena in which the new schools of social theory are

interested – in particular language and the interpretation
of meaning'
(All quoted passages are from ibid., p. xvi)

Despite the fact that this starting point commits him to a
position closer to the earlier than the later Parsons, Giddens'
representationalism is rationalistic rather than empiricist. That
is, for both of them theory originates in theory and in particular
in their conceptions of the current state of theory. Moreover,
for Giddens if not for Parsons, who after *The Structure of Social
Action* was a far more original theorist on this score, the building
blocks of theory are previous conceptualisations. Thus Giddens
makes his argument by either positively restating or defining his
position against, in order: Freud, Erikson, Goffman, Hagerstrand, Foucault, Collins, Durkheim, Marx, Blau and many
instances of what he terms 'evolutionary theory'. This is
because for him, regardless of how they were actually produced
and in a remarkably explicit if not self-conscious manner, they
either provide more or less well-formed parts of the picture that
he needs to complete what he clearly regards as his theoretical
jigsaw, or, as in the cases of Foucault, Blau and evolutionism,
they represent fragments of alien puzzles against which he
contrasts his own.

For Giddens, then, theory does not originate in the
encounter with a resistant reality as it did for his classical
predecessors. He describes the latter activity as concerned with
'establishing and validating generalisations' and demotes it to
the status of 'only one among various other priorities or aims of
social theory' (ibid., p. ix). Thus he says: 'Social theory has the
task of providing conceptions of the nature of human social

activity and of the human agent which can be placed in the service of empirical work' (ibid., p. xvii). One of the sources, then, of Giddens's representationalism lies in his pre-realist view that there are only two modes of theorising, both representationalist: a rationalist mode, which defines his project, and an empiricist mode which, while perfectly proper, defines the project of under-labourers who would be best advised to accept the direction of the master theorists. Thus instead of social-scientific development being the product of, as it is for ordinary realism, a continuous, undivided and craft-like alternation between the abstract and concrete moments of theorising, for Giddens it is a Taylorised activity wherein some draw up plans and others try to match them using the materials to hand.

Another source of Giddens's representationalism is the ontological humanism apparent in the passages quoted above to specify his starting point. Not only is the 'active, reflexive subject' to be the focus of his imaginative but avowedly palimpsestic labours, but also language is understood (contra Saussure) as the product of such subjects. The subject's centrality is confirmed when Giddens suggests that the empiricist and structuralist traditions have both missed the fact that two types of generalisation are possible in the social sciences: the first type hold 'because actors themselves know them . . . and apply them in the enactment of what they do' (ibid., p. xix), while the second type 'refer to circumstances . . . of which actors are ignorant and which effectively "act" on them, independent of whatever the agents may believe they are up to' (ibid., p. xix).

The humanism of this point becomes explicit as Giddens elaborates on it. For he goes on to argue that the first type of generalisation should be privileged since the assumption of the 'knowledgeability of agents' is central to his restating of 'conceptions of human being and human doing, social reproduction and social transformation' (ibid., p. xx). Moreover, the elision of the human and the social to the ontological advantage of the former that is suggested by this quotation is confirmed when Giddens continues by announcing that what defines structuration theory is its reading of the 'linguistic turn' as an event of ontological rather than epistemological significance. Thus, with respect to ontology, he consciously adopts and radicalises precisely what I regard as the self-contradictory or non-position located earlier in Bhaskar (see above, p. 18): the subject/object distinction must be transcended as an anachronistic dualism and replaced by a conception of 'the duality of structure' (ibid., p. xxi):

> Human social activities, like some self-reproducing items in nature, are recursive. That is to say, they are not brought into being by social actors but continually recreated by them via the very means whereby they express themselves *as* actors. In and through their activities agents reproduce the conditions that make these activities possible (ibid., p. 2).

Because it rules out in advance the possibility that there may be forms of social life other than and other to human actors or entities reducible to them that are responsible for social reproduction, this formulation of our ontological condition begs at least two questions. First, 'What does bring "human social activities" into being?' Second, 'How is knowledge possible given that there is no permissible moment of subject/object separation?'

81

These questions do not detain Giddens until Chapter 4 so they need not detain this presentation until it reaches said chapter. The reason for this is, as he says, that the concept of the 'duality of structure' 'leads directly to other main themes, especially that of the study of time–space relations' (ibid., p. xxi). Indeed it does and to a clear declaration of his representationalism too. The more 'substantive part of the volume', Chapter 2, begins with a breathtaking example of sociological arrogance or naïvety – the revising of psychoanalytic 'ego psychology' to stress the role of habitual activity in constraining the unconscious. This habitual activity involves a 'positioning of the body' not simply in 'immediate circumstances' but also in the 'seriality of encounters across time–space'; that is, in the 'life-span', 'institutional time', the '"supra-individual"' structuration of social institutions', and the 'multiple way[s] . . . conferred by specific social identities' (all quotations from ibid., pp. xxiv–xxv). Additionally, the 'contexts of social interaction' are also positioned relative to one another or 'regionalised'. In Chapter 3 the representationalism implicit in this focus on what is directly picturable is made explicit by Giddens' declaration that the method of structuration theory should be an enhanced version of Hagerstrand's 'time–geography' with its 'time–space maps'.

Amongst other things, Hagerstrand's maps depict 'agents . . . [moving] in physical contexts whose properties interact with their capabilities . . . at the same time as those agents interact with one another' (ibid., p. 112). This becomes the core of Giddens's concept of structure except that, in a way reminiscent of Parsons inclusion of 'means and conditions' within the 'unit act', he specifies 'rules and resources' as the 'physical contexts' of agents. This, then, is the way that social structure disappears from his theory – reduced to rules and resources made or assembled by other or preceding actors in time–space. In the same way, Lockwood's distinction between social and system integration is necessarily transmuted into two kinds of social integration: face to face relations and non-face to face relations (ibid., pp. 376–7). The communication of the nature of the concept of structure that remains almost defeats even Giddens's formidable grasp of the signifiers:

> Structure, as recursively organised sets of rules and resources, is out of time and space, save in its instantiations and co-ordination as memory traces, and is marked by an 'absence of the subject'. The social systems in which structure is recursively implicated, on the contrary, comprise the situated activities of human agents, reproduced across time and space. Analysing the structuration of social systems means studying the modes in which such systems, grounded in the knowledgeable activities of situated actors who draw upon rules and resources in the diversity of action contexts, are produced and reproduced in interaction (ibid., p. 25).

In Chapter 4 Giddens, literally, fleshes out the significance of this conception. Logically determined by his humanism, all senses of the constraint that Durkheim argued was evidence for the *sui generis* character of the social are restated as the results of human action, including those cases where human agents 'are unable to do anything other than conform' (ibid., p. 178). This said, Giddens nevertheless wishes to argue that there is always a certain patterning to human action, to the nature of 'rules' and the access to 'resources', which 'allow[s] recognizably consistent forms of time–space distanciation' or the '"stretching" of social systems across time space' (ibid., p. 181). The resulting 'structural principles' – 'Tribal Society', 'Class-Divided Society' and 'Class Society' – are instantiated in institutions ('structural properties') which routinise the human actions necessary to sustain social life in different ecological settings; that is, according to whether the population is distributed into 'bands', divided between the 'city and the countryside', or exists in a 'created environment' (ibid., pp. 180–5). The theoretical significance of these categories is then demonstrated by a rewriting of Marx's account of the central institutions of capitalism and his more general concept of contradiction in these terms. The chapter concludes by arguing that such a rewriting allows a far greater sensitivity to the possible ways in which human beings may make history than Marx was able to display.

Here, in sum, is further support for my general contention that theorising outside of a programme of ongoing substantive research – and Giddens has never engaged in such a programme – is likely to result in a representationalist theoretical practice. Giddens neatly summarises the ocularcentrism of his epistemology as follows:

'Societies', then, in sum, are social systems which *'stand out' in bas-relief* from a background of a range of other systemic relationships in which they are embedded. They stand out because definite structural principles serve to produce a specifiable overall 'clustering of institutions' across time and space (ibid., p. 164, emphasis added).

Here too is the answer provided by structuration theory to the first of the begged questions identified above and concerned with what brings human social activities into being: the things and thoughts preceding generations and co-existing actors left or leave lying around. The second begged question, namely that concerned with how knowledge is possible given that no moment of subject/object separation is permissible is not answered, save of course, unconsciously, by the privileging of theoretical vision.

In providing this account of Giddens's theory, and except in one regard, it has not thus far been my intention to be critical of his logic, nor even to suggest that, in so far as I have provided an accurate representation of his theory, he would be surprised by anything that I have said. Save, of course, for its corollary which is that, for reasons beyond his control, his theory is therefore both intellectually anachronistic and likely to be substantively banal (see Chapter 3). My more immediate purpose has simply been to establish that he theorises in a rationalistic and therefore representationalist manner. This, however, is also something that might surprise him since one of his most fundamental criticisms of prior efforts to theorise structure is that it 'is often naively conceived of in terms of visual imagery, akin to the skeleton or morphology of an organism or to the girders of a building' (ibid. p. 16). Naive though these images may be, to their users among the classical theorists they were simply metaphors which, as I hope I have shown in the preceding chapter, they moved beyond with their actual conceptualisations. Thus my major criticism of Giddens's logic is that so far from moving beyond such visual metaphors, he has in fact simply and literally given them flesh. For what else is his cartographic conception of social structure as an entity existing in space–time but a restating of Durkheim's ecological morphology of population but with a visible human skeleton or physiology instead of Durkheim's invisible social-structural one?

As Giddens himself seems to indicate when he says that 'structure... is out of time and space, save in its instantiations and co-ordination as memory traces' (ibid., p. 25), social structure is for him a theoretically necessary virtual entity. It is, in sum, none other than the metaphor that guides his theorising. Ironically, then, the ghost in Giddens's mental machine is the very concept he wishes to dissolve. This suggests three things. First, another logical flaw in Giddens's argument since one ought not to reject the assumption that makes one's thought possible. Second, as a corollary, even structure's spectral presence means that it must provide the criteria against which Giddens's efforts have to be judged – of course, on these criteria his efforts fail because his theory is not intended to confirm the existence of social structure as a *sui generis* entity. And third, if even its most implacable foe depends upon a concept of social structure in order to think through his effort to dissolve it, then it must indeed have something going for it.

Giddens's, and indeed many of his readers', inability to recognise the regressively representationalist nature of his practice in providing us with his version of the theory that Parsons never gave us represents a serious setback which has already had unfortunate consequences for theoretical work and substantive analysis. As regards theoretical work, his example has greatly strengthened the belief that Nietzsche warns against in the first of the quotations which the present study opens, namely the idea that theorising is a palimpsestic activity and therefore merely a matter of, reading, restating or, worse, bowdlerising or simply summarising and commenting upon other people's theorisations at great length which is guided by fashion rather than any theoretically generated logic. Hence Giddens's own chasing of terms originating in but seldom credited to the theoretical or research programmes of others, like risk, reflexivity, the 'third way' (Rose, 1999), and modernity (see below, Chapter 3). Giddens' consequent difficulties in articulating his concepts with substantive observations are made embarrassingly clear in the course of his recently published conversation with the doyen of British economic journalists, Will Hutton (Hutton and Giddens, 2000). I will make my case with respect to his equally regrettable effect on the quality of some substantive analysis in the next chapter. These consequences, however, are only in part a reflection of his great influence among younger sociologists and cultural studies academics.

Another factor in their explanation is a parallel failure on the part of those who should know the dangers of representationalism but apparently do not. In general terms, this is the failure of those who have propagated idealist readings of post-structuralism which not only allowed the highly subjectivist nominalism that is postmodernism to flourish, but also led to the unavailability of any rigorous statements of the non-representationalism that is the one certain antidote to postmodernism. When contrasted to the postmodernists and indeed earlier sociological Wittgensteinians like Peter Winch (1958), Giddens's stress on the visible, acting and not simply thinking human substance of the social makes him seem like a realist. However, he is not a realist and the fact that he may appear to the untutored to be one is simply a striking further testament to the power of Saussure's insight as to the paradigmatic and oppositional nature of the production of meaning.

HALL AND THE MUDDLE OVER REPRESENTATION

Of all the idealist readings of post-structuralism that are around, I have chosen to focus on that produced by Hall. This is for several reasons. First, he is as, if not more, influential than Giddens, especially in Cultural Studies. And second, he has written at greater length than any of the alternative candidates about the problem of representation. A consideration of Hall's theoretical work on representation confirms the element in my first rule of neo-classical method which refers to engagement in a programme of ongoing substantive research as being a necessary *but not a sufficient* condition for the production of non-representationalist theory. This is because, despite the fact that Hall has been continuously involved in substantive work – directing and/or co-writing major studies of youth culture, street crime, racism, the media and Thatcherism, as well as engaging in numerous pieces of cultural analysis – there is a very substantial weakness in his understanding of the nature of representation itself.

The text I will discuss here is his opening chapter in the Open University textbook, *Representation: Cultural Representations and Signifying Practices* (Hall, 1997c). Hall begins by distinguishing three different theories of language: the 'intentional', which is what I term rationalist representationalism; the 'reflective', which is what I refer to as empiricist representationalism; and the 'constructionist', which is his term for a combination of Saussure and Foucault's theories.

The discussion of these theories is preceded by a discussion of the meaning of the term 'representation' which makes it clear that for Hall, while words stand for concepts of things, they are also used to refer directly to those things. This, then, is where my problems with the text begin since signification and reference are not clearly distinguished as different operations requiring separate understandings. On the contrary, Hall comments that representation involves giving 'meaning to *things* through language' (ibid., p. 16, emphasis added). The point is later reinforced when he says:

> *In the first place*, then, meaning depends on the system of concepts and images formed in our thoughts which can stand for or 'represent' the world, enabling us to refer to things both inside and outside our heads (ibid., p. 17, emphasis added).

> Meaning depends on the relationship between things in the world – people, objects and events, real or fictional – and the conceptual system, which can operate as *mental representations* of them (ibid., p. 18, emphasis in the original).

> We are able to communicate because we share broadly the same conceptual maps and thus make sense of or interpret the world in roughly similar ways ... That is why 'culture' is sometimes defined in terms of 'shared meanings' (ibid., p. 18).

> However, a shared conceptual map is not enough. We must also be able to represent or exchange meanings or concepts,

and we can only do that when we also have access to a shared language. Language is therefore the second system of representation involved in the overall process of constructing meaning (ibid., p. 18).

To place such an account of representation before that of the different theories of language was a fateful decision. Not only does Hall's account of representation conflate the production of meaning with the achievement of reference and so pre-decide much that is at issue between the competing linguistic paradigms, but it also pre-decides what is at issue in favour of the rationalist variant of the representationalist paradigm, which is the opposite of what Hall appears to have intended.

To elaborate: first, when Hall discusses the theories of language, he makes it very clear that he has no time for the intentional (rationalist) and reflective (empiricist) approaches that are the two poles of the representationalist paradigm but instead strongly favours the constructionist approach. Second, despite the formal accuracy of his presentation of the component elements of Saussure's theory, he misses one vital aspect of its significance for the understanding of the nature of representation: namely, that meaning is produced *in* language by the operation of syntagmatic and paradigmatic relations in bringing signifiers and signifieds into alignment with one another. In other words, meaning is not something that in any sense is pre-existent relative to language as Hall would have it. Rather, as Saussure states, the signifier and the signified have the same mutually defining quality as the recto and verso of a sheet of paper. Third, Hall's major criticism of Saussure is that he provides no theory of reference. This, then, raises the question of where Hall's understanding of it comes from. He briefly but positively mentions the American Pragmatist, Pierce, in this connection, before repeating the latter's, and unknowingly confirming his own, unintended, rationalist representationalism in the following way: '[w]hat Saussure called signification really involves *both* meaning and reference' (ibid. p. 34, emphasis in the original). On the contrary, in my view it cannot possibly also involve reference since, as Saussure says, the relationship between signs and their referents is arbitrary. Moreover, if 'language is radically powerless to defend itself against the forces which from one moment to the next are shifting the relationship between the signified and the signifier' (Saussure, 1974, p. 75), how could it possibly defend itself against the even more diffuse forces determining reference?

In sum, then, Hall unintentionally remains within the representationalist problematic despite his Saussurian vocabulary in that he rationalistically regards concepts as pre-linguistic, mental pictures of real or imagined worlds that are communicated through language. This is the result of him neither understanding that within the significatory paradigm meaning is produced in language, nor acknowledging that within the same paradigm reference *has* to be distinguished from signification. In the light of the latter failing in particular, it is not at all surprising that, throughout the long and again formally accurate account of Foucault's conceptual development that Hall later provides, there is no acknowledgement that Foucault provided a theory of reference let alone a new visuality, a new way of understanding and producing representations. Had he done so, he would have realised that the social significance of representation extends way beyond what even the text *Representation* as a whole suggests, which is simply the entirely common-sensical idea that it is part of the regulated production of consumables that may have significance for the supposed identities of certain social groups.

CONCLUSION

I am in no position to judge the effects of Hall's confused reading of significatory theory on his more specific cultural analyses. However, I do think that it is possible to argue that it has affected his more general substantive work in such a way that it has provided a surprising opening for both postmodernist and Giddensian attempts to dissolve any sense of social structure that has its source in substantive research. This argument is set out in the following chapter which focuses on the symbiotic role of Giddens and Hall's rationalistic representationalisms in giving what I regard as a wholly regrettable currency to the term 'modernity' and its cognates in contemporary sociological and political discourse.

CHAPTER THREE

Myopia and Modernity

The bourgeoisie cannot exist without constantly revolu-tionising the instruments of production, and thereby the relations of production, and with them the whole relations of society. Conservation of the old modes of production in unaltered form, was, on the contrary, the first condition of existence of all earlier industrial classes. Constant revolutionising of production, uninterrupted disturbance of all social conditions, everlasting uncertainty and agita-tion distinguish the bourgeois epoch from all earlier ones. All fixed, fast-frozen relations, with their train of ancient and venerable prejudices and opinions, are swept away, all new-formed ones become antiquated before they can ossify. All that is solid melts into air, all that is holy is profaned, and man is at last compelled to face with sober senses, his real conditions of life, and his relations to his kind (Karl Marx and Friedrich Engels, 1967, pp. 45–6, emphasis added).

Marx's writing is famous for its endings. But *if we see him as a modernist*, we will notice the dialectical motion that underlies and animates his thought, a motion that is open-ended, and that flows against the current of his own concepts and desires. Thus, in *The Communist Manifesto*, we see that the revolu-tionary dynamic that will overthrow the *modern bourgeoisie* springs from that bourgeoisie's own deepest impulses and needs:

> *The bourgeoisie cannot exist without constantly revolutionising the instruments of production* (Marshall Berman, 1982, p. 20, emphasis added).

> *As Marx said about modernity*, '[it is a] constant revolutionising of production, uninterrupted disturbance of all social relations, everlasting uncertainty and agitation . . . . All fixed, fast-frozen relations, with their train of ancient and venerable prejudices and opinions, are swept away, all new-formed ones become antiquated before they can ossify. All that is solid melts into air (Stuart Hall in Hall *et al.*, 1992, p. 277, emphasis added).

> *By equating capitalism with modernity*, and working-class struggles with non-sectarian, progressive interests . . . *Marx failed to grasp* two central matters: first, that there are forms of politics which cannot be understood from the perspective of class alone; and, secondly, that a 'critical' account of modernity must embrace a far wider perspective than labour interests if it is to claim to represent 'a humane and just social order' (David Held summarising Giddens, in Hall *et al.*, 1992, p. 34, emphasis added).

In the progression between these passages one may observe some of the effects of the return of rationalistic representationalism within social theory, namely the erasure of Marx, capitalism, class and ontological depth from contemporary sociological discourse. The result has been the onset of a rather pronounced theoretical myopia which has meant that much contemporary theory sees no further than the governing common sense allows – that is, the focus determined by the latter has been tightened rather than slipped in anyway. In the first passage, Marx talks with his customary care about one of the conditions of the *bourgeoisie*'s continuing existence. In the second, Berman tentatively suggests that Marx might have anticipated some of the insights of the aesthetic modernists of the later nineteenth century. In the third, care and caution are cast aside and Marx is presented, ostensibly on the basis of the very same quotation, as a theorist of all of something now called 'modernity'. And in the fourth, the *coup de grâce* is delivered as Marx is condemned for equating capitalism with modernity and not knowing about our present social movements!

In what follows, and with apologies to a current pop celebrity, I wish to question the general sociological utility of the master concept formerly known as capitalism – Modernity. That is, I wish to challenge the advisedness of the substitution that is supposedly justified by the train of thought that informs the progression between these passages.[1] In my view, the term 'modernity' returned to sociological discourse after an absence of some fifteen years or so simply as a reflex response to the talk of postmodernity. Its return is regrettable since 'modernity' either has no sociological meaning, since all it means is something like 'the way things are today', or if it does have such a meaning it takes one of two equally unacceptable forms.

In one case, certain cultural developments such as the Renaissance, Cartesianism, the Enlightenment, or the rise of individualism are specified as defining modernity. This may or not be justifiable if one is concerned simply with cultural history, but when it is extended to the social sphere as a whole it

necessarily instances an idealism which is as often unacknowledged and unjustified as it is sociologically unacceptable.
Relatedly but in this case entirely irrelevantly, the term has,
of course, long been a latent element in historiographical
discourse – *vide* the growing popularity of the term 'modern
history' during the nineteenth century to refer to the period
between the 'culture wars' of the mid-seventeenth century, in
which the Moderns finally defeated the Ancients in the struggle
for intellectual dominion (Bury, 1920, Ch. 4), and the onset of
'contemporary history'.

In the other case, and this is the meaning whose particularly
baleful consequences I will spell out below, it is defined in a
more plausibly sociological way that has its origins in a very
particular and now hegemonic representation of American
society. This is the representation provided by sociologists
like Daniel Bell (1960, 1967) and David Riesman (1950), which
was given a technologically determinist inner logic by the
eponymous Modernizationists of the 1960s (Levy, 1966, for
example). This representation identified the combination of
liberal democracy, a capitalist economy, an open class structure, and an individualistic value system as the antithesis of
totalitarianism whether fascist or communist. Not the least
of the reasons for making this claim was the fact that so many
modernist artists and intellectuals had fled Europe for the
United States. This suggested to Bell *et al.* that the latter
provided the context most conducive to the aesthetic current
that they regarded as representing the quintessence of human
freedom (Alexander, 1995, pp. 10–19; Brick, 1986). In this
way, then, an aesthetic concept became a sociological one since
the term modernity was thenceforth used to name Bell *et al.*'s

representation of American social reality. Hence my use of the term Social Modernism to refer to their thought and the wider political ideology, with its core signs of 'self-reliance', 'opportunity', 'responsible unionism' and 'loyalty', that both constituted and was constituted by it (Woodiwiss, 1990a, Ch. 8, and 1993).

In sum, my argument begins by insisting that the genealogical relation between social modernism/modernity, on the one hand, and aesthetic/philosophical modernism, on the other, is the reverse of what it is generally assumed to be. That is, contra Kumar (1995, Ch. 4) and many, many others, rather than believing that a general social condition that had long been called modernity produced an aesthetic movement, I believe that an aesthetic signifier became a sociological one under the very particular and relatively recent social circumstances instanced by the United States in the 1950s. The conclusion that I will seek to justify below, therefore, is that whenever the terms modernity and, by extension, postmodernity are used in general *sociological* discourse their effect is an unwarranted historical retrojection and/or global projection of the Social Modernist conception of American society in the 1950s. These effects are sociologically and politically regressive. This is because in replacing 'capitalism' with 'modernity' as they have sought to overcome economic essentialism, many of today's leading social thinkers have embraced: 1) an analytical framework that avoids rather than solves the critical sociological problem of how the different structural orders relate to one another; and 2) a post-Whig metanarrative (change without the possibility of betterment is the fate of humankind) that pictures the last four or five hundred years of *world* history as culminating in a set of structural arrangements and political aspirations that an earlier generation of sociologists – the Modernizationists – imagined had superseded capitalism in the United States during the 1950s.

Moreover, as I will demonstrate below, there are good reasons for thinking both that today's neo-modernizationists do not realise that this is what they are (they condemn Modernization Theory far more often than they praise it), and that the return of 'modernity' is part and parcel of the return of representationalism. The result is that much of what passes for the 'cutting edge' of contemporary social theory looks more like an instance of a postmodern artefact than an attempt to understand the provenance and significance of such things. That is, it displays much of the apparent delight in fragmentation, eclecticism and pastiche, as well as the depthlessness, the nostalgia and the utopianism, if not the sometimes saving self-ironising quality, which characterises such artefacts (Jameson, 1991, Ch. 1).

The chapter ends by suggesting that we restore the conceptual prince, capitalism, to its rightful position of pre-eminence within sociological discourse, albeit in the context of a new, non-representationalist theoretical settlement that recognises the validity of many of the claims made by the very poststructuralism that is thought by some to have provided the principal supports for the new sociological currency of 'modernity'.

HABERMAS, GIDDENS AND THE RETROJECTION OF 'MODERNITY'

As far as I know, not one of the founding troika of sociology ever gave the term modernity or its cognates any sociological content. Thanks to the labours of the one contemporary scholar who has taken the trouble to investigate the sociological genealogy of the term, David Frisby (1985), we know that it was Georg Simmel who first gave it some sociological content. However, as Frisby's very careful study also makes clear, what Simmel meant by the term related more to a particular aspect of his present – 'the fleeting, transitory and the fortuitous' (ibid., p. 20) – than to its overall structure and historicity. Thus Simmel is the critical link between the earlier aesthetic and philosophical usages to be found in the works of Baudelaire and Nietzsche and the later 'cultural studies' of Benjamin, Kracauer and the wider Frankfurt school.

This is the usage that Habermas (1981, 1987a, 1987b) and Marshall Berman (1982) rediscovered and, prompted by the Modernizationists but otherwise purely by analogy (that is, without direct textual support), extended to the founding troika. In Habermas's case especially, this extension was over-determined by his strong negative reaction to post-structuralism and postmodernism, which appears to have driven him to find value (albeit for his own distinctive reasons) in almost any-thing that they disparaged. This double origin creates diffi-culties, however. The first is that those whom I will refer to slightly misleadingly as the Simmelians do not mean the same thing by modernity as either the postmodernists or such critics as Habermas. Thus the inescapability of the 'fleeting, etc.' sits rather awkwardly beside a scientistic 'metanarrative' preaching 'truth' and 'progress' in Habermas's thought. The former calls for an inter-rogation of social surfaces, while the latter has always pointed to supposedly underlying metaphysical struc-tures (cf. Jay, 1985, p. 126). The second difficulty is that while

Simmelians like Benjamin define the social-structural sources of this condition in more or less Marxist terms as capitalism, the postmodernists do not investigate its social-structural sources at all, save to say that, self-contradictorily, they are something to do with technology and are more than a matter of economics (see below, p. 138).[2]

Habermas attempts to overcome these difficulties in a rationalistically representationalist manner by seeing the two definitions of modernity as pointing to contradictory aspects of a larger whole. And he sees this larger whole as the 'unfinished project' initiated by Hegel, namely the *neuzeit*'s (questionably, Habermas regards Hegel's term *neuzeit* as a synonym for 'modernity') need 'to create its normativity out of itself' (Habermas, 1981, p. 7) – a need which has been frustrated by the capitalist-inspired domination of a scientistic 'instrumental reason'. He therefore deprecates the efforts of those, the American Modernizationists in particular, who would reduce modernity to:

> the formation of capital and the mobilisation of resources; to the development of the forces of production and the increase in the productivity of labour; to the establishment of centralized political power and the formation of national identities; to the proliferation of rights of political participation, of urban forms of life, and of formal schooling; to the secularisation of values and norms; and so on (ibid., p. 2).

Habermas's main problem with the Modernizationists is that, by severing the connections between these processes and the larger project of the 'need to create its normativity out of itself', they have 'contributed to the currency of the expression "post-modern"', since they have made modernity into something that could have lost contact with its origins and may therefore be exhausted. One of my problems with Habermas is that, apart from this difference and because he otherwise reasonably rejects economic determinism, he accepts and thereby gives plausibility to the Modernizationists' fragmented picture of modernity's social-structural or 'systemic' character. For reasons that will become clear below, I will briefly interrupt this discussion of Habermas to say something about Giddens's work in this area.

As with so many other modish terms, it was Giddens who first gave a wider sociological currency to the term modernity after Habermas and Berman had reintroduced it into the sociological lexicon. After *The Nation-State and Violence* (1985), when the term suddenly (cf. *The Constitution of Society*, 1984) turns up unexplained on page one to differentiate his approach from Marx's, he never looked back. In the 1985 book, however, there is little to suggest the extent of his coming rapprochement with Modernization Theory, except for his use of the term 'industrialism', and his acknowledgement that it refers to technological effects which are not identical with or reducible to those of capitalism as a set of social relations. Otherwise, his account of the 'institutional clusters associated with modernity' (Giddens, 1985, pp. 310ff.) retains a rhetorical *marxisant* edge, including as it does references to 'class', 'surveillance' and 'military violence' as the other significant clusters. However, by 1990 and the publication of *The Consequences of Modernity*, these 'clusters' had been placed within a clearly modernizationist problematic with which they were somewhat at odds:

How should we identify the discontinuities which separate modern social institutions from the traditional social orders? Several features are involved. One is the sheer *pace of change* which the era of modernity sets into motion. Traditional civilisations may have been considerably more dynamic than other pre-modern systems, but the rapidity of change in conditions of modernity is extreme. If this is perhaps most obvious in respect of technology, it also pervades all other spheres. A second discontinuity is the *scope of change*. As different areas of the globe are drawn into interconnection with one another, waves of social transformation crash across virtually the whole of the earth's surface. A third feature concerns the *intrinsic nature of modern institutions*. Some modern social forms are simply not found in prior historical periods – such as the political system of the nation state, the wholesale dependence of production upon inanimate power sources, or the thoroughgoing commodification of products and wage labour (Giddens, 1990, p. 6, emphasis in original).

In this passage, not only has 'modernity' been reunited with its modernizationist twin, 'tradition', but its supposedly distinctive dynamism is stressed, as is 'the wholesale dependence of production upon inanimate power sources'. All of this points firmly in the direction of unacknowledged modernizationist sources such as the following:

My definition of modernization hinges on the uses of inanimate sources of power and the use of tools to multiply the effect of effort (Levy, 1966, p. 11).

Nevertheless, like (following?) Habermas, Giddens insists on the insufficiency of such characterisations of modernity and its significance. Also like Habermas, Giddens sees the ultimate significance of modernity's arrival as the difference it made to the way in which time is conceptualised. Habermas talks of 'modernity's consciousness of time' and invokes Reinhart Koselleck's (1985) work, the main thesis of which he summarises and comments upon as follows:

> Modernity's specific orientation toward the future is shaped precisely to the extent that societal modernization *tears apart the old European experiential space* of the peasant's and craftsman's lifeworlds, mobilizes it, and devalues it into directives guiding expectations. These traditional experiences of previous generations are then replaced by the kind of experience of progress that lends to our horizon of expectation (till then anchored fixedly in the past) a 'historically new quality, constantly subject to being overlaid with utopian conceptions'. Yet Koselleck overlooks the fact that the notion of progress served . . . to close off the future as a *source* of disruption . . . . In Benjamin's view, historicism . . . [organizes] the objectified course of history into an ideal simultaneity in order to fill up *'empty and homogeneous time'* (Habermas, 1987b, p. 12; emphasis added).

Similarly but apparently *ex nihilo*, Giddens (1990, p. 20) specifies what is distinctive about modernity as 'time–space distanciation', which he refers to as a product of:

> the *separating of time and space* and their formation into standardised, *'empty'* dimensions cut through the connections

between social activity and its 'embedding' in the particularities of contexts of presence . . . . A *standardised dating system*, now universally acknowledged, provides for an appropriation of a unitary past (emphasis added).

Again like Habermas, Giddens (ibid., p. 21) indicates a preference for this way of differentiating the modern from the traditional as compared to what he almost but never quite refers to as the modernizationist ideas of 'differentiation' and 'functional specialisation'. He then goes on to specify two types of 'disembedding mechanisms': 'the creation of symbolic tokens' and 'the establishment of expert systems' (ibid., p. 22). His discussion of the former focuses on money and this connects his interest in 'modernity' with the Simmelian tradition (but very superficially), while his discussion of the latter simply emphasises that, as exemplified by traffic lights(!), they have become taken-for-granted aspects of our social environments. Both mechanisms disembed 'by providing 'guarantees' of expectations across distanciated time–space' (ibid., p. 28), and so give a special analytical salience to concepts which in my view sit very uneasily with Simmel *et al.*'s stress on the 'fleeting', namely Luhmann's (1993) categories of 'trust' and 'risk'. The latter are categories which owe much of their prominence in Luhmann's work to the need to find a way of talking about cross-system linkages whose existence is otherwise denied by his insistence on the autopoeisis of differentiated functional sub-systems.

That said, it should also be pointed out that a somewhat more developed, but again entirely rationalistically representationalist, theory of 'modernity' may be found in Luhmann's work than in that of the Modernizationists who inspired him. For

Luhmann, insofar as social systems cohere they do so not because of the effects of a shared value system but simply because, notwithstanding their autopoietical character, every sub-system is an aspect of every other sub-system's environment or, to use another analytical language, is an element in their conditions of existence. However, more because it is too rigorously non-humanist than because it is too plainly analogical, Luhmann's systems theory in general holds even fewer attractions for Giddens than it does for Habermas (Luhmann and Habermas, 1971). Be that as it may, Giddens approaches the end of his unacknowledged and unargued repetition and amalgamation of Habermas and Luhmann's points by stating, again like Luhmann, that what above all differentiates modernity from tradition is the specific character of the 'relation between modernity and reflexivity' (ibid., p. 36):

> With the advent of modernity, reflexivity takes on a different character. It is introduced into the very basis of system reproduction, such that thought and action are constantly refracted back upon one another (ibid., p. 38).

Giddens completes this version of his ever-changing theoretical collage by stating that his characterisation of modernity points to more than enough sources of change and instability to account for our supposed present sense of unease without resorting to categories such as postmodernity. For Giddens and Habermas the inequalities and injustices that because of capitalism continue to mark the social relations of modernity are the most obvious and scandalous signs of the incompleteness of the modern project. It is difficult, however, to see how their representationalist and more modernizationist than Simmelian discussions of modernity could contribute to the illumination of the ways in which these scars are institutionally reproduced – at least in any way that improves upon the classically rooted account of Benjamin (see Berman, 1982 and Frisby, 1985, Conc.). Moreover, in neither case is there any serious interrogation of the social surface. Instead, Habermas talks in a deep 'modernist' register, about the institutional suppression of the 'communicative reason' that the arrival of modernity made possible. And Giddens (1990, Chs 2 and 3) talks in a depthless, descriptive and tautological way about how 'disembedding', etc. can help us to understand the significance of the globalisation of capitalism and industrialism; that is, globalisation leads to the spread of deformed trust and risk relations. What makes Giddens's contribution 'depthless' is certainly not any lack of thought or seriousness on his part. Rather the depthlessness of his analysis (like Bell's more recent work, see Woodiwiss, 1993, pp. 111–20) is an unintended by-product of 'overcoming' economic determinism in a representationalist, modernizationist or Luhmannesque manner by simply adding other supposedly equally perceptible determinative spheres to the economy and dispensing with the idea that when one talks of these spheres one is talking of invisible but imbricated and interpenetrative entities and causal processes that we can only know through their visible effects. The result, in line with Giddens's general refusal to sustain any sense of social structures as *sui generis* phenomena (see above pp. 83–6); and Craib, 1992), is the disappearance from his work of any acknowledgement of what Bhaskar (1978) has termed 'ontological stratification'. Hence the ever more pronounced shift from the analytical to the descriptive register in his conceptual language as his work has developed. Whatever their cause, it seems to me that it is the minimalist nature of the explanatory gains made by Habermas and Giddens that accounts for the fact that the wide dissemination of their ideas has had the profoundly ironic consequence that the most obvious sign of their influence is the renewed currency not just of the modernizationist vocabulary but also of the values that it carries – values that are antithetical to their own.

HALL AND THE GLOBAL PROJECTION OF MODERNITY

Habermas instances Critical Theory's self-conscious coming to terms with modernization theory and Giddens instances a semi-conscious rapprochement on his own behalf. Despite the fact that his values too are antithetical to those carried by modernizationism, some of Hall's recent work instances a wholly unconscious rapprochement on the part of the Structuralist/Marxist camp. One obvious reason why the fact of Hall's rapprochement might be especially deeply repressed in his own discourse is because Marxists had been particularly critical of modernisation theory in the 1960s and 1970s, especially in the area of development studies (see Harrison, 1988). However, Hall's apparently unknowing adoption of significant elements of the modernizationist rather than Simmelian sense of 'modernity' seems to me to be a most telling indicator of the fateful significance of both Habermas and Giddens's naturalisation of the modernizationist vocabulary and the more general regression to representationalism in social theory.

On the opening page of Hall's introduction to the Open University's flagship sociology text, *Formations of Modernity* (1992), he declares that he will use the 'common-sense term "modernity"' to refer to his object of interest – a surprisingly naive statement on the part of so accomplished a student of discourse, who indeed later refers to the term's 'contested discursive history'. Especially surprising since on the very same page he immediately goes on to prepare the way for his later deployment of the modernizationist concept of differentiation by arguing that the 'multi-causal approach' he is about to outline renders all 'mono-causal' approaches anachronistic. Thus the four major social processes that he identifies – 'the political, the economic, the social and the cultural' (Hall and Gieben 1992, p. 1) – are treated 'as different processes working according to different historical time-scales'. Moreover, the emergence of such distinct domains is one of the main markers of modernity. The analytical results are twofold: first, economic determinism and idealism are all right provided that they are confined to the analysis of the economic and cultural domains respectively; and second, any possibility of understanding the interrelationships between them is closed off. Thus the 'defining features or characteristics of modern societies' are listed as follows:

1 The dominance of secular forms of political power and authority and conceptions of sovereignty and legitimacy, operating within defined territorial boundaries, which

are characteristic of the large, complex structures of the modern state.

2 A monetarised exchange economy, based on the large-scale production and consumption of commodities for the market, extensive ownership of private property and the accumulation of capital on a systematic, long-term basis. (The economies of eastern European communist states were an exception to some of these features, though they were based on the large-scale industrial production and consumption of goods.)

3 The decline of the traditional social order, with its fixed social hierarchies and overlapping allegiances, and the appearance of a dynamic social and sexual division of labour. In modern capitalist societies, this was characterised by new class formations, and distinctive patriarchal relations between men and women.

4 The decline of the religious world view typical of traditional societies and the rise of a secular and materialist culture, exhibiting those individualistic, rationalist and instrumental impulses now so familiar to us (ibid., pp. 6–7).

Now, it takes remarkably little in the way of deconstructive labour to uncover the substantive similarities between this picture of society and that basic to modernisation theory. I use the term 'picture' because, although Hall presents his definition as a 'conceptual model', it is in fact, like the modernizationist original, the product of a process of blinkered historical generalisation which, notwithstanding Hall's possible arguments to the contrary (ibid., p. 7), must be intrinsically representationalist. My point is that despite any differences of intellectual formation, including prolonged exposure to the non-representationalism associated with post-structuralism, whenever one seeks to present the institutional silhouette of the societies that are commonly taken to be modern on the basis of observable characteristics, one ends up with an utterly conventional modernizationist and therefore vision-dependent representationalist picture of such societies (cf. Luhmann, 1982, p. 193). This is a picture that privileges the nation state, emphasises exchange over production relations in the economy, contrasts the fluidity of the new social relations to the supposedly fixed nature of those that preceded them, and discusses cultural change in terms of a shift from a religious world view to a secular and individualist one. It is also a picture which, because of its particularities and especially its insistence on differentiation, has a clear affinity with the Social Modernist characterisation of 1950s America as comprising: an autonomous, pluralistic polity which functioned neutrally to allow the aggregation, expression and equitable satisfaction of interest group demands; a non-exploitative, rationally directed and largely self-contained post-capitalist economy; an open class/stratification system that functioned, again autonomously, to ensure that the most demanding social roles are filled by the most able players supported by a kinship system that, likewise, functioned to ensure that the mainly male role players are physically and psychologically fit to perform their roles; and finally, an individualistic if not wholly secular value system that socially and psychologically validated and integrated all the self-directed striving required by the various autonomous sub-systems.

The simple presentation of the archetype should be sufficient to make one highly sceptical of any schemata based upon it. But if it is not, a consideration of its fate at the hands of subsequent generations of critically-orientated American sociologists and social historians should do the trick. And not simply because they have exposed the falsity of many of its claims (to equal opportunities, the eradication of poverty and democracy for all, for example), but also because it was the manifest implausibility of its assumption as to the autonomy of the separate spheres which for a time gave Marxist class theory a definite plausibility in the United States, notwithstanding the numerous deficiencies that we are now so well aware of. However, to confirm the results of my little deconstruction, there is no mystery as to why Hall should have produced such a picture since, as he indicates (op. cit., p. 7), the basis for his generalisations is the extant comparative and therefore largely secondary literature, much of which is structured by modernizationist assump- tions and concepts, and therefore must fail to acknowledge the resistant phenotypical differentness of even Western European societies let alone such non-western ones as Japan.

The result is that Hall's 'defining features', like the modern- izationist originals, are either, as in the case of his characterisa- tions of the political and economic domains, so abstract as to be devoid of analytical content or, as in the case the charac- terisations of the social and cultural domains, so specific as to be Ameri-centric. A further result is that if one attempted to use Hall's model to compare, say, Japan and the United States, one would end up saying (as indeed he indicates, ibid., p. 10) that politically and economically they are the same, while socially and culturally Japan is pre-modern for two reasons. First, the 'fixed hierarchies and overlapping allegiances' characteristic of, for example, its corporate life have tended to pre-empt the emergence of a 'dynamic social and cultural division of labour'; and, second, its traditionalist culture has tended to pre-empt any thoroughgoing individualism. These would not be very interesting statements. This is because they repeat those made by Japanese Marxists (Hoston, 1987) in the 1930s and by modernizationists in the 1960s (Morley, 1971, for example). They are also highly misleading. Even a cursory reading of a decent newspaper should make it clear that the political and economic differences between Japan and the United States are also extremely significant. In addition, a somewhat more attentive reading of the more specialist literature should make it clear that Japan's culture is not 'strikingly traditional' as Hall misleadingly describes it – in no other society that I know of has tradition been so assiduously and continuously re-invented (Woodiwiss, 1992). All of which suggests at least one reason why modernization theory's lack of ontological depth is so problematic – it prompts not only a misleading reading of the significance of visible 'phenotypical' characteristics but also an equally misleading focus on them to the exclusion of invisible 'genotypical' ones. This last, in turn, leads to false comparisons and contrasts, as a consequence of which, for example, the United States could be thought to share more with the former Soviet Union than with Japan.

In sum, the evidence for thinking of Hall's model as a repetition of its modernizationist predecessor is almost exactly the same as in Giddens's case (see above, p. 104). First, the emphasis on differentiation (even more complete and enthusiastic on Hall's part than on Giddens's). Second, the presence in his model (see above, p. 108–9) of such explicit traces of Modernizationist discourse as the invocation of the 'logic of industrialism' in the bracketed section of the second defining characteristic, the tautologous usage of the terms 'modern' and 'traditional', and the deployment of such once famously vague buzzwords as 'large-scale' and 'dynamic'. And third, the commitment to a set of definitional criteria that have evolutionistic consequences, intended in the Modernizationists' case but most definitely unintended by Hall and Giddens.

What confirms the specifically unconsciousness character of Hall's repetition is the fact that he goes to some pains to distance himself from Modernization Theory. However, if one looks closely at his critique, it quickly becomes apparent that it is the suggestion that the driving force behind differentiation is economic in character to which he objects (ibid., p. 10), rather than either the overall structure of the modernizationist model or even the idea of economic determination as such. The nature of the modernizationist model is never specified (as significant a silence as Giddens's odd inability to acknowledge explicitly his borrowings from it?) and, as indicated earlier, the autonomy of the different domains is supposedly basic to sophisticated contemporary sociology. In other words, Modernization Theory is discussed and dismissed in order to balance, but more importantly to reinforce, his critique of Marxism.

So much, then, for why Hall has no problem with determinisms – they save him from a determinism. And so much also for how his acceptance of determinisms opens his text to Modernizationist discourse – it too assumes the differentiation of the different domains of the social. What I would like to do now is to turn to the question of why he, like many social theorists today, would feel so little discomfort in the face of any critique that stressed their difficulties in relating the different structural orders to one another. Here it is necessary to draw attention to the fact that Hall's critique of Marxism is every bit as partial as his critique of modernization theory. Hall accepts the post-structuralist critique of the common-sense sociological assumption that concepts are to be understood as empirical representations of the extra-discursive realm, although it should be noted that he presents this critique with a very strong interpretivist and therefore idealist accent (Hall *et al.*, 1992b, pp. 10–11). However, he fails to see that his own concepts are produced in an equally representationalist way, as Hall was inadvertently to confirm in his later text on representation (see above, pp. 88–92)

Thus, although because of his entirely commendable desire to escape from economic essentialism, he talks of domains rather than levels of analysis, Hall identifies these domains with different concrete institutional formations or, echoing Giddens, 'organisational clusters' (Hall *et al.*, 1992a, p. 11). In this way, then, he strongly implies that these domains are understood to be as separate in reality as they are in theory, although because of his latent idealism he suggests that what they will look like will vary with who is doing the representing. Of course, Hall insists that these domains interact with one another at the macro level and so define the particularities of specific social formations. However, when it comes to the micro level, Hall's representationalism has the following consequences. First, this level is conceptualised humanistically rather than 'structurally' (that is, as consisting solely of interactions between individuals, rather than as involving relations between structures at different levels of abstraction – for example social formation and workplace (see Woodiwiss 1990a, Ch. 2). Second, these individuals are understood to be positioned solely by the effects of discourse on their identities, and therefore, on Hall's reasoning, by the cultural domain alone. That is, they cannot be understood as positioned by the political, economic, and class/gender domains, since for Hall (like many Critical Theorists, but contra Giddens, 1984, p. 33) these neither possess a cultural dimension, nor have a presence at the micro level (Hall *et al.*, 1992b, p. 277).

The results, then, of Hall's representationalism are threefold. First, he continues to regard *the* sociological problem as the conventional Hobbesian problem of order (that is, as concerned with the understanding of the irrepressible tension between individuals and society). Second, he does not so much reject determinisms as reject determinism. And, third, because he works with a fragmented representation of society rather than because of a thoroughgoing non-representationalism, he comes close to fully accepting postmodernism's stress on the supposedly fragmented nature of social (and individual) reality (Hall *et al.*, 1992b, p. 10). That is, having said that the different domains interact with one another, he cannot specify how this occurs, since to do so would require him to acknowledge not only that they are either actually imbricated with one another or, as in the case of class, the product of such imbrication across the institutional spectrum, but also that they are interpenetrative of one another.

Before I specify the consequences of Hall's strange route to postmodernism for the sense he makes of the equally uncovenanted arrival in his text of large fragments of Modernizationist discourse, I would like to consider where all this leaves him as regards the concept of class – ill at ease I would think.

Class, at least in the surprisingly empiricist form of general-isations about 'class formations', retains an important place in his thinking as one of the 'defining features . . . of modern societies'. Indeed, together with 'patriarchy' and to the again surprising exclusion of racism and much else besides, class is implausibly presented as exhaustive of what Hall puzzlingly regards as the specifically social dimension of sociality. In the sociological classics class is understood as a concept that syn-thesises the economic, political and economic dimensions of the social, albeit in Marx's case on terms set by an underly-ing economic essentialism. This, however, does not appear to be how Hall understands it. Instead, because of his representa-tionalism he appears to conceive of class too as an autonomous and irreducible domain – what class formations might be, if they are not in some sense syntheses of economic, political and ideological/cultural relations, he does not make clear. Perhaps he would agree with Luhmann that class is a survival of an earlier (that is, pre-functional) form of differentiation? I have written at length elsewhere (Woodiwiss, 1990a) about how I think one may combine an acknowledgement of the autonomy and irreducibility of the different dimensions of sociality with a synthetic and therefore, in explanatory terms, modest concep-tion of class, and so I will not go into it now. I mention Hall's awkwardness concerning class here simply to make the point that, since it is not a synthetic concept for him, it causes him no difficulties in his only slightly hesitant race to embrace the postmodern stress on fragmentation.

If he were consistent, Hall's social modernist theoretical unconscious would have prompted him to read the changes that occurred in Britain during the 1980s as the belated achievement of a state of supposed high modernity equivalent to that attained in the United States in the 1950s. Instead, he takes them as indicative of the imminent arrival of postmodernity (note that Giddens is truer to his social modernist unconscious when he speaks of our present condition as 'radicalised modernity'). To develop these points, the American Social Modernists of the 1950s argued that the advent of their local variety of advanced, democratic capitalism – with its minimalist welfare system, its routinised industrial relations, its large 'middle class', its acknowledgement of the social salience of issues related to 'race' and gender, its consumerism, and its privileging of the quest for individual autonomy – falsified the predictions of, in particular, the ideologists of the American Left and so signified 'the end of ideology'. In an uncannily similar way, the British social modernists of the common room, think tanks and New Labour advisory groups, much of whose pre-governmental conversation Hall makes explicit, can be heard some thirty years later to have argued that exactly the same characteristics of advanced, democratic capitalism have falsified the predictions of the ideologists of the British Left (that is, of themselves in their earlier political incarnation) and so signify the occurrence of 'the end of ideology' here too (see Hall *et al.*, 1992b, Intro.).

Unaware though Hall and those he may have spoken for may be of the iterative character of their discourse, it is nevertheless not difficult to see both how it was possible and why the term postmodernity should have displaced modernity within it. To summarise, the iterative character of Hall's discourse is an inter-textual effect made possible by his unconscious representationalism and brought about by the profound but unacknowledged influence of modernizationist sociology on

117

the secondary theoretical and substantive literature upon which it depends. The displacement of the term modernity by that of postmodernity was similarly a palimpsestically produced intertextual effect, but this time one brought about by a combination of Hall's past Marxism, which is what perhaps allowed him to think that he could not possibly mean the same as the Modernizationists even when he used their vocabulary, and the forgetting of Social Modernism that marks the more recent texts of those, like Daniel Bell (1973, 1976), upon whom Hall depends for his sense of an imminent postmodernity. In sum, then, what forces Hall into the repetitive mode is a textual unconscious that is formed by, but denies, the connections between the discourse of Social Modernism, its forgetting, and academic postmodernism – if social betterment is impossible, so too is intellectual/aesthetic progress, since all talk of progress depends upon claiming a knowledge of the invisible and the structural that was seen as implicitly totalitarian and even somewhat demonic. Confirmatively, the net effect of the denied relationship is the same in Hall's text and the wider discourse it exemplifies as it had been in the United States – the impossibility of attention to, let alone anger at, capitalism as a system of production, especially on the part of former Marxists it seems.

BAUMAN AND THE RETURN OF SOCIAL MODERNISM

In order to make explicit the most likely normative and therefore political consequences of the analytical trajectory I have been describing, I will end by discussing the final chapter of Zygmunt Bauman's *Intimations of Postmodernity* (1992). This is because the impossibility of attention to and anger at capitalism becomes clear, even if it still remains implicit, in his account of why it is necessary to respond positively to calls such as Crook *et al.*'s (1992) for a return to the 'social action' problematic (a response which remains latent in Hall's texts in the form of his interest in an idealist and largely humanist concept of 'identities'). In the course of a long and always highly readable intellectual journey, Bauman has made his debts to Habermas, Berman and Giddens, if not to the Modernizationists, very clear with respect to his understanding of modernity. He is also a lot less hesitant than any of the writers discussed above when it comes to naming and defining our present condition. For him our condition is undoubtedly postmodern. What this means for him, perhaps intentionally echoing as well as agreeing with Habermas, is that at last 'modernity [is] for itself'. What he means by this, unintentionally echoing Social Modernism, is that there is now supposedly a general recognition that what critical sociologists once considered to be the signs of modernity's failure (its continuing pluralism, differences, contingency and ambiguity) are now understood to be its successes. And for this reason Bauman is prepared, not only to declare that postmodernity has arrived as a global social condition, but also, somewhat surprisingly, to legislate as to the stance that sociologists who wish to understand this condition should take. Thus, like Crook *et al.*, he argues that we must 'reverse the structure of the cognitive field' (Bauman, 1992, p. 190) and focus on 'agency' and its 'habitats' rather than structure and its systematicity.

The inter-textual effects of interest to me in Bauman's book are not so much those that connect the concepts of 'agency' and 'habitat' with the Parsonian action schema, although they are self-evident, as those which connect the same concepts with the social ideology that the Parsonian schema validated (Robertson and Turner, 1991, *passim*), namely Social Modernism. Thus, in the first of what he terms the 'main tenets of the theory of postmodernity', Bauman restates his commitment to the primacy of 'agency' in postmodern society and sociology, before, in the second, commencing his unconscious repetition of 1950s' Social Modernism by declaring postmodern societies to be already part of what Marxists term 'the realm of freedom'. In the third and fourth of his tenets, Bauman directly repeats in relation to the present two of the fundamental Social Modernist claims about the United States of the 1950s. That is, he states that under postmodern conditions agents are for the most part self-reliant actors who are free to pursue the opportunities that their habitats provide. In the fifth of his tenets, he speaks (in terms that recall Reisman's famous distinction between 'inner direction', 'other direction' and 'autonomy') of the consequences for agents of the extreme motility of a society defined by the pursuit of opportunity as a move from the pursuit of long-term 'life projects' to engagement in a life-long process of 'self-constitution'. In the sixth, seventh and eighth of his tenets, Bauman identifies what I am sure he would not acknowledge as the homeostatic processes that hold what otherwise appears to be a dangerously centrifugal system together. The first of these is the responsibility of agents for their own self-disciplining – albeit exemplified by reference to 'body cultivation' rather than organised labour as in Social Modernist discourse! And the second is the loyalty of the actors – Bauman speaks of their 'self-proclaimed allegiance' (ibid., p. 195) – to '*symbolic tokens* of belonging' (emphasis in the original), which reassure 'the agent that the current results of self-assembly are indeed satisfactory' (ibid., p. 195). These tokens gain their necessary 'authority' because of the 'expertise' of those that proclaim them and/or (in terms that call to mind McCarthyism) because of their 'mass following'. Finally, as in Bell's version of Social (Post)Modernism (see Woodiwiss, 1993, p. 115), the repressive possibilities implicit in the last point are blandly denied when Bauman states that, whatever it may have been in the past, the most important symbolic token today is 'information' (ibid., p. 96).

So here, then, is an explicit if once again unknowing claim that the same characteristics (validated as self-reliance, opportunity, responsibility and loyalty) that supposedly made the United States the first modern society, today justify the contention that the United States and many other societies are instances of postmodernity. Here too is a repetition of the claim that these are the characteristics of the good (or as good as you can get) society.[3] What, of course, makes the representation of contemporary Britain in these terms appear to be more plausible than it deserves to be is the fact that, as Hall ([Hall and Jacques] 1985, 1988) above all has taught us (albeit without making the American connection), precisely such a representation informed the Thatcherite project. Aside from the fact that so-called postmodern societies are overall even more unequal and unpleasant than 'modern' America was, my main objection to these claims is that they are metatheoretically as well as sociologically banal:

the only difference between a banal theory and a fatal theory is that in the former the subject always believes itself to be more clever than the object, while in the latter the object is always taken to be more clever, more cynical, more ingenious than the subject, which awaits it at every turn (Baudrillard, quoted in Poster, 1989, p. 198).

This is hardly a surprising result since, as Nicos Mouzelis (1991) and John Holmwood (1996) made clear in their anticipations of the argument developed in Chapter 2, social theorists have for too long ceased to be sociologists, that is to be engaged in the business of empirical research for explanatory purposes. Indicatively, whereas the Modernizationists were named after what they had 'discovered', the postmodernists have (perforce?) narcissistically named what they have 'discovered' after themselves.

CONCLUSION

The net result is that, because of their rationalistic representationalism, several of the leading sociologists of our day, like their American forebears, have mistaken a real and significant change in some dominant representations of some national social realities for a change in the whole of global social reality. Moreover, in spite of their otherwise rampant eclecticism, they have in many cases entirely deprived themselves of access to the body of concepts summarised by the term 'capitalism', and in all cases deprived themselves of the insight as to the ontologically stratified nature of social reality that these concepts carry. Thus they combine a largely unintended and certainly not Simmelian concern for social surfaces with an eclecticism and a fascination with fragmentation, all made possible by a nostalgic recuperation of a happier social theory and topped off with an increasingly pronounced utopianism.[4] For this reason, then, it seems to me that much of their recent work may be rather precisely referred to as a symptomatic of the influence of post-modernism, rather than as an attempt to explain the social conditions within which it flourished.

Finally, the substitution of 'modernity' for 'capitalism' as a general sociological descriptor has not had the beneficial effects that its proponents hoped for. Instead because, as Derrida and Foucault have taught us, no term in any talk, let alone 'serious talk', stands on its own, there has been a regrettable change in both Sociology's central signifier and the concept of the discipline's object that it projects. The economic reductionism with which the concept of capitalism has most often been conjoined is clearly unsustainable and all the writers discussed above have contributed to this realisation. Why then do they not realise that they reproduce the effects of just such a reductionism when they repeat the modernizationist formula? Even if one forgets the latter's patent technological reduction-ism, and provided, of course, that one thinks that there is more than one modern/postmodern society in the world, use of this formula means that one believes that (for reasons that are never/can never be specified) certain technological and eco-nomic structures have always been accompanied by certain political and cultural ones, or vice versa. In fact, despite the capitalisation of many aspects of their economic relations, many societies continue to exhibit many significant social-structural differences when compared to some supposed 'Western' arche-type. Contra Giddens (see above p. 104), Japan, like many Moslem countries, has even maintained its own calendar. For most domestic purposes this is not in any sense the empty sig-nifier 2001, but very definitely *Heisei* 13 (that is, the thirteenth year in the reign of the *Heisei Tenno*), and many documents not so dated are of very questionable legal validity. Thus to talk of globalisation as modernisation is to be guilty of Ameri- or Euro-centrism, as Giddens (1990, Ch. 6) has in fact shown himself to be uneasily but in the end unapologetically aware.

My view is that we can now avoid such arrogance without giving up on the possibility of a universalisable social science, given that we are free of economic essentialism and, thanks to the post-structuralists, could be free of representationalism. However, this will only happen if we give up the inevitably culturally tainted 'ocularcentric' search for a general descriptor, and create a theoretical apparatus purged of ethnocentrism as our way of generating our representations of the world. More-over, at least until such time as the economic inequalities intrinsic to capitalist economic relations have markedly less of a structuring effect in other spheres and in the world as a whole than they have currently, we should talk of '*capitalism*' or '*capitalisms*' when we wish to talk of national or transnational social formations. 'Capitalism' because it has rigorously if variously defined signifieds whose referential plausibility and explanatory power in relation to social relations are well-established. And 'capitalisms' because the larger, constitutive, environing and irreducible national and transnational structures of which these relations are necessarily a part are always different.

CHAPTER FOUR

Visuality after Postmodernism

The present chapter has four main parts. The first very briefly outlines the development of Postmodernism and explains how I too came to take it at least a little seriously by critically reflecting on my own teaching practice. The second clarifies what is meant by theory and outlines the postmodernist critique of what it considers to be the pretensions of contemporary social theory. The third introduces Jay's typology of the 'scopic regimes of modernity' and discovers a marked and unfortunate similarity between the 'visuality' of the Postmodern and that of the seventeenth-century Baroque. The fourth argues that Foucault's archaeological concepts, specifically those of the discursive formation and the rules of formation of a discursive formation, provide us with a new but hitherto neglected theory of reference and therefore with the basis for a genuinely new way of understanding how we visualise the social and what our reflexive methodological responsibilites are.

WHAT WAS POSTMODERNISM?

As the intellectual dust raised by Postmodernism settles, it is becoming easier to discern its shape and assess its sociological significance. Postmodernism first emerged as an only partly self-conscious aesthetic stance that, beginning in the early 1960s, challenged the orthodoxies of modernism in the arts. Its practitioners rejected the modernist commitment to seeking after and attempting to represent the true or deeper nature of things by developing new and distinctive modes of representation in favour of working on found images and mixing styles (*vide* the contrast between Surrealism and Pop Art). It gradually became a more intellectually self-conscious movement as it entered the academy (especially departments of Architecture, Art History and Literature) and became linked with a particular and most often idealist reading of such post-structuralist writers as Roland Barthes, Jacques Lacan, Jacques Derrida and Foucault. These writers were regarded as radicalising the significance of Saussure's rejection of the representationalist paradigm in Linguistics, and therefore as stressing, each in his distinctive way, the positive analytical benefits of the actual or possible uncertainty of meaning consequent upon the mutual irreducibility of signifiers, signifieds and referents. If painting could no longer be judged on the basis of its verisimilitude, nor could any other instance of communication.

With the publication of Lyotard's *The Post-Modern Condition* in 1979, the movement became a fully self-conscious, pan-disciplinary 'anti-foundationalism' that claimed to have transcended metaphysics as such (that is, all ontologies and epistemologies). It thus saw itself as a sign of times defined by a generalised 'incredulity towards [the] metanarratives' that had hitherto underpinned the quest for knowledge (see below, p. 135–7). In close to this form, although certainly not under the label of Postmodernism, it had already entered sociology as a critique of epistemology (Hindess and Hirst, 1977) and potential solvent of class theory (see, Cutler *et al.*, 1977; Cottrell, 1984; Johnston, 1986; Hindess, 1987; and, critically, Woodiwiss, 1990a, Ch. 8). It was also soon to become a foundation (irony intended) for much of what has become known as Cultural Studies, wherein it unfortunately became the required position if one wished to be regarded as taking the cultural sphere plus issues of 'race', gender and sexuality seriously. These days, because all of the authors of its primary texts have refused to identify themselves as postmodernists, it exists only in secondary texts and textbooks as an unauthorised but nevertheless largely unchallenged idealist reading of the unfortunate primary authors. Until very recently, despite numerous disavowals on the part of its progenitors (most recently Derrida, 1994), the most obvious way in which such garden-variety postmodernism announced its presence in sociology was by Marx-trashing. In this role it has regrettably been highly successful (witness the displacement of the term 'capitalism' by that of 'modernity' as a general descriptor across a wide range of sociology texts published after about 1985, see Chapter 3 above). I say 'regrettably' for two reasons. First, the consequences of this trashing have been theoretically and substantively disappointing – some well-deserved but hardly novel criticism of economic reductionism but little that is constructive. Second, the idealist and therefore generally anti-sociological character of the readings through which the original post-structuralists have become known to a wider audience has lost them a large number of potential readers who might otherwise have put their ideas to more constructive use.

Because my work is an attempt at such constructive use from a realist and indeed *marxisant* sociological position and thus will appear profoundly counter-intuitive, not to say self-contradictory, to many readers, it is perhaps now necessary for me to make some very brief but perhaps overdue comments concerning two points at even this early stage of this chapter (I will elaborate on both points in considerably more detail below). The first point concerns what is positive about post-structuralism from my point of view. And the second concerns the possibility of a contradiction. What is positive about post-structuralism may be easily explained. And it is simply that, thanks to the non-representationalist or significatory concept of language upon which it rests, it provides both a way of appreciating the autonomous life of discourse and a method for investigating it – two things that are notoriously absent from the sociological and especially the Marxist tradition. This said, the one proviso that must be entered is that post-structuralism's distinctive insistence upon giving a new significance to the linguistic and language-borne dimension of social life should also be registered metatheoretically at the epistemological and not simply at the ontological level as has most often been the case hitherto. Put briefly, this is because, if the specificity of language as an instrument as opposed to an object of under-standing is not acknowledged, language is likely to be regarded as the ineffable source of both the world and its understanding. For this reason the difference between the world and what is thought about it becomes very hard to maintain. The erasure of this difference creates problems not simply because it violates the key realist metaphysical postulate that the world exists whether or not human beings think about it, but also because in so doing it also removes the possibility of error (Bhaskar, 1978; Trigg, 1981). Where the world and thought about it are not

128

considered to be identical, the possibility of error is ever-present, as is, by the same token, the possibility of truth. And it is what Garry Potter (1999) has aptly termed the 'bet' on the latter possibility which saves realists from the theoretical paralysis that otherwise appears to follow from the verificational scepticism in relation to claims about the nature of the extra-discursive world that they share with the postmodernists as well as the post-structuralists. In sum, the critical methodological lesson to be learnt from the post-structuralists is not that the world is a linguistic construct but that knowledge should be pursued in a non-representationalist manner. Its significance is therefore transformative with respect to established disciplines which, as Derrida (1990, p. 933) likes to put it, have their 'proper idioms', rather than formative with respect to the pro-duction of a new discipline.

The conditions that make it possible to combine, for example, elements of classical sociological and Foucaldian theory with-out involving oneself in metaphysical self-contradiction may also be put briefly for now. Elements of the two theories may be combined without contradiction provided: 1) that, to extend Althusser (1969), one reads classical theory as a non-humanist; and 2) that one refuses those postmodernist/idealist readings of Foucault that present his work as denying the independent subsistence of the social. In short, given these provisos, both positions may be seen to be instances of non-humanist onto-logical and epistemological realism; that is, as granting the social its independent subsistence, acknowledging the necessity of the articulation of language and observation in the intellectual appropriation of that reality, and insisting on the impossibility of any claims to certainty (see also, Pearce, 1988).

HOW I CAME TO LOVE
POSTMODERNISM (ALMOST)

Somewhat surprisingly, the nineteenth-century Parisian *flâneur*, whom Charles Baudelaire and, following him, Walter Benjamin both saw as an archetypally modern figure because of the pleasure he took in wandering the city's streets and shopping arcades, has become a postmodernist hero (Tester, 1994). I say surprisingly because, for Benjamin (Buck-Morse, 1991) at least, a twentieth-century *flâneur* such as himself was engaged in revolutionary activity. This was the uncovering of the wonderfully rich and profligate material 'ur-culture' of capitalism. And the reason such activity was revolutionary was because its purpose was to make the proletariat once again aware of the promise of abundance that is implicit within capitalism but denied to them by its social relations of production. This said, I have to admit that, personally, I am something of a postmodernist *flâneur* in that I enjoy shopping for its own sake and am often thoughtlessly enthusiastic about my purchases.

A case in point would be when I bought a copy of a feminist text by Rosi Braidotti entitled *Patterns of Dissonance*. It is I am sure a splendid book but my knowledge of it, I am ashamed to say, remains limited to a table that I noticed as I flicked through it. This had been copied from an earlier text by Michèle Le Doeuf. The table and its immediate context read as follows:

In the list of Pythagorean oppositions (given in Hegel's *Lectures in the History of Philosophy*, vol. 1), one finds the following:

limit and infinity
unity and multiplicity
masculine and feminine
light and dark
good and evil

This list (and the associations which it suggests) is probably not out of date (Braidotti, 1991, p. 193).

Facing the prospect of what seemed like the impossible task of summarising the differences between classical and postmodernist social theory to a final-year class the following week, this table and Braidotti's encouraging comment on its current pertinence seemed like manna from heaven. Without going into detail I will simply say that it worked brilliantly as a way of summarising the contrasting representations of the social provided by the two bodies of theory. What was more, it not only had the imprimatur of two leading feminist theorists but also that of a philosophical heavyweight of great venerability — perhaps I had stumbled on an eternal truth and in any event the students were greatly impressed. Eternal verity or not, I forgot about it until the time approached when I had to give the same class the following year. This time though I thought I had better check the original source in order to understand how this remarkably prescient table had been arrived at.

I turned first to Hegel's *Lectures* where I found the full list which read as follows:

1 The finite and the infinite
2 The odd and the even
3 The one and the many
4 The right and the left

5 The male and the female
6 The quiescent and the moving
7 The straight and the crooked
8 Light and darkness
9 Good and evil
10 The square and the parallelogram (Hegel, 1892, pp. 215–16)

For Hegel, this table was one of the sources of the dialectic which may or may not be a worthwhile and rationally defensible idea. But for his own mystically inspired, numerological reasons Pythagoras had had to find 10, no more and no less, oppositions. Hence, or so it seemed to me, the desperation evidenced by the inclusion of items 2, 4 and 7. In any event, this was enough for me to begin to be concerned about the authoritativeness that I had allowed my students to grant to the edited table the previous year. As a result I enquired further into Pythagoras's beliefs. In Bertrand Russell's *History of Western Philosophical Thought* (1961, p. 50) I discovered that Pythagoras founded a religious order whose rules included the following:

1 To abstain from beans
2 Not to pick up what has fallen
3 Not to touch a white cock
4 Not to break bread
5 Not to step over a crossbar
6 Not to stir the fire with iron
7 Not to eat from a whole loaf
8 Not to pluck a garland.
9 Not to sit on a quart measure
10 Not to eat the heart

11 Not to walk on highways
12 Not to let swallows share one's roof
13 When the pot is taken off the fire, not to leave the mark of it in the ashes, but to stir them together
14 Do not look in a mirror beside a light
15 When you rise from the bedclothes, roll them together and smooth out the impress of the body

Russell wryly comments in introducing this list:

> [this] religion . . . here and there, acquired control of the State and established a rule of the saints. But the unregenerate hankered after beans, and sooner or later rebelled.

There would be no justice in belabouring Pythagoras in any more detailed terms, besides he had some other ideas – notably that of structure – that have stood the test of time better than any of mine will. My point is that I invoked his authority and selectively quoted from him to solve my own problem with a class. In other words, it was in this way, and all the more affecting because of its banality, that two of the postmodernist's points finally came home to me: first, their point about the imbrication of power and knowledge – with two leading feminists, Hegel and Pythagoras backing me up, how could the students disagree; and second, their point about judging ideas by their usefulness rather than by their provenance – the table had after all worked very well as a pedagogic device.

WHAT IS SOCIAL THEORY?

Whenever I ask student or seminar audiences to write down the first word that comes into their heads on hearing the term 'social theory', their answers generally fall into one of just two categories – either they suggest negative associations as in the cases of 'chaos', 'conflict', 'abstraction' or 'complexity', or they identify it with a particular body of theory such as 'functionalism' or 'Marxism'. Similarly, when I then go on to ask them to define social theory in as simple terms as they can, their answers are typically anything but simple and sometimes take a long time to provide. However, when I then ask them what they would bring me if I asked them to fetch a piece of theory, they rapidly move on from suggesting a book to telling me what I want to hear, namely that it consists of words organised as sets of definitions or concepts. Likewise, when I ask what distinguishes theoretical definitions from the ordinary ones to be found in dictionaries, they are also quick to state that the former stand in a more rigorously defined relationship to the aspects of the world to which they refer than the latter.

With somewhat less alacrity but little real difficulty student audiences can also be brought to recognise two further things. First, that this rigour is a product of the (claimed) observance of certain metaphysical or metatheoretical rules, namely those that pertain to matters of ontology and epistemology, matters of substance and matters of method. And second, that it is the varying nature of these rules that accounts for many of the substantive differences between concepts and theories that ostensibly refer to the same realities. For example the fact that Edward Thompson (1964) worked with a humanist ontology and an empiricist epistemology explains much about why his account of class relations is, and even looks, so different to that provided by Nicos Poulantzas (1975) who based his work on non-humanist and realist metatheoretical assumptions.

Finally, once students become aware, through using and discussing their answers to the self-assessment questionnaire reprinted as Figure 2, that not only do they themselves not agree on what the proper metatheoretical basis for social-scientific enquiry should be, but also that two such masters from the same theoretical tradition cannot agree, they become able to appreciate the force of the postmodernist critique of what the latter term 'modernist social theory'. That is, they can see the force, first, of the postmodernist's argument that, because of the undecidability of the issues it addresses, metatheory does not provide the foundations of scientificity so much as those of a Tower of Babel. Second, what also appeals is the postmodernists' explanation for the modernists' capacity to continue to believe they are engaging in an intellectually privileged activity called science despite all the counter-indications provided by the evidence of metatheoretical chaos that is all around them.

The latter is the explanation provided most clearly by Lyotard when he argues that, whatever their differences, all modernist thinkers share a belief in at least two *grands récits* (metanarratives) which he terms the Myths of Progress and Truth. The first of these refers to the belief that the pursuit of knowledge is good in itself and should ultimately lead to a better world, while the second refers to the belief that the true nature of the world is knowable. Within the justificatory context provided by these two metanarratives, the current chaos within social theory simply reflects temporary problems and cannot detract from the fact that everything remains to be played for. For Lyotard though, this persistence is foolish and potentially dangerous. For him the metanarratives of truth and progress are myths in a strong cognitive sense in that both are demonstrably false. The

Ask yourself or the texts you are reading the following questions:

Ontological questions (What sort of thing is being investigated?)

	1	*2*	*3*
a) Does it depend on us thinking about it for its existence?	yes	no	no
b) Is it a material object (i.e. accessible to our senses)?	no	yes	yes
c) Are people the object of interest?	no/yes	yes	yes/no

Epistemological questions (How should it be investigated?)

	1	*2*	*3*
a) Should one begin with observation?	no	yes	no
b) Should one ever reason without reference to observations?	yes	no	yes (to a degree)
c) Is certainty possible?	yes	yes (to a degree)	no

Final question

How would you explain the links between the answers to the ontological questions and the answers to the epistemological ones?

Key: 1 = idealism/rationalism; 2 = empiricism/positivism; 3 = realism
Where double answers (e.g. no/yes) are given the first is the most common within the tradition.

NB The three metatheoretical traditions indentified above are not the only ones to have ever existed but they do comprise the basic ingredients out of which all others have been created. Thus interpretivism and symbolic interactionism are combinations of an idealist ontology and an empiricist epistemology, while the more sophisticated variants of 'garden variety' postmodernism are a combination of a realist ontology with an idealist epistemology.

How to criticise the present author: he answers as a straight down the line realist for whom people are not the primary object of sociological enquiry. Thus you can begin to unravel his argument by simply disagreeing with any one or more of his answers and drawing out the consequences for the main argument of the present text.

Figure 2 How to identify a metatheoretical position

inherently progressive nature of the pursuit of knowledge is falsified by the role of social and natural science in the great crimes of the twentieth century: the Holocaust, the Gulags and the creation of weapons of indiscriminate, mass destruction. Also, the belief that the true nature of the world is ultimately knowable is no longer accepted by those who are supposed to know about these things, namely the philosophers of science – he instances Thomas Kuhn (1970) in particular. Moreover, according to Lyotard he is not the only one who knows the modernist metanarratives to be false since it was the spontaneous spread of such scepticism from the 1960s onwards that enabled him to describe our condition as now postmodern. In the light of this transformation in our condition, he avers that it would be best if we accepted that our sciences were simply a variety of 'language game' with no superior status to any others and therefore to be judged solely according to their utility in solving practical problems. In other words, we should be brave and try to find a way of, as others have put it, reasoning without foundations or illusions. Above all, we should be modest.

Now much as 'modesty' appeals to me as a watchword, albeit for a realist's rather than a postmodernist's reasons, I cannot accept Lyotard's reasoning. This is not because I do not accept the role played in legitimating scientific activity by the meta-narratives of Progress and Truth. Not only do I accept that they play this role but also I accept that they are both mythic and have sometimes been dangerous. The reasons for my scepticism towards the sceptics have to do instead with my non-acceptance of some of the assumptions upon which their case rests. First among these is their substantive sociological assumption – necessary if knowledge is regarded as having become purely a matter of will – that the cultural or discursive realm either has always been or has recently become autonomous from such other dimensions of sociality as the economic and the political. For Lyotard this autonomy is largely a function of computerisation, while for Jean Baudrillard it is the product of some two hundred years of the multiplication and sophistication of images and their production. The latter is a process that has reached its apogee in the current impossibility of any un-*mediated* experience and the consequent desire for simulations of the real that have taken us into the realms of the hyperreal and virtual reality. As Baudrillard (Poster, 1989, p. 171) says of Disneyland:

[It] is the perfect model of all the entangled orders of simulation. To begin with it is a play of illusions and phantasms: pirates, the frontier, future world, etc. This imaginary world is supposed to be what makes the operation successful. But, what draws the crowds is undoubtedly much more the social microcosm, the miniaturised and *religious* revelling in real America, in its delights and drawbacks . . . . In this imaginary world the only phantasmagoria is in the inherent warmth and affection of the crowd, and in that sufficiently excessive number of gadgets used there to specifically maintain the multitudinous affect . . .

The objective profile of the United States, then, may be traced throughout Disneyland, even down to the morphology of individuals and the crowd. All its values are exalted here, in miniature and comic-strip form [emphasis in the original].

There are at least three ways of undermining the culturalist assumption that underpins the understanding of our present predicament implicit in this passage. The first is to challenge it directly and substantively in the way that Frederic Jameson (1991), David Harvey (1989) and I (1993) have done in our different but complementary refusals of any notion that the arrival of the hyperreal involves the supercession of capitalism. The second is to point out as many others have done that it leads to the self-contradictory statement that the truth is that there is no truth. The third is not simply to identify the metatheoretical assumption that it reintroduces into social-theoretical discourse as idealism, but also to show how this happens. It is to the latter part of the third mode of criticism that I will now turn. This is not so much because I consider it to be particularly damaging to the postmodernist's claims to novelty, although it is, but more because it enables me to begin to advance my own positive agenda for a recuperative transformation of social theory. This, in turn, is because it involves challenging the postmodernists at the level of their assumptions about the nature of language, which was precisely the point at which they felt most secure in their sense of superiority *vis-à-vis* so-called modernist social theorists. In sum, what I will demonstrate below is that, whereas the postmodernists claimed to work with a post-Saussurian conception of language and despite their distrust of all modes of representation, they in fact only succeeded in reinforcing the hold of the representationalist paradigm over social science.

SCOPIC REGIMES

In order to do this, I have to introduce another and what Lyotard might refer to as a 'figurative' dimension of metatheory, namely that represented by what Jay (1988; 1993) has termed the 'scopic regimes of modernity' (see also, Crosby, 1997; Lowe, 1982). Lying behind the idea of scopic regimes and what makes them almost literally figurative as well as in a certain sense prefigurative is the distinction between 'vision' and 'visuality'. That is, as indicated in my Introduction, what allows the notion of scopic regimes is the recognition that vision is not a spontaneous power in the way that common sense supposes when it tells us that 'seeing is believing' and when it generally exalts sight over all the other senses. Rather it is a constructed power as the many doubters of sight's trustworthiness have suspected for as long as common sense has exalted it. This constructedness is what is registered by the use of the term visuality instead of vision (see the many excellent essays collected in Levin, 1993).

The significance of this distinction in the present context is that when the veracity of vision is not called into question, it is commonly accompanied by or even leads to a representationalist understanding of the nature of language and therefore of the status of concepts. Whereas when vision's social-constructedness is acknowledged it generally points, but only points, in the direction of a Saussurian or significatory understanding of the nature of language and concepts. Moreover, these possible linkages between understandings of vision and understandings of language and concepts may be either strengthened or weakened by the other metatheoretical assumptions with which they are entwined. Thus, simply because human beings are visible, a humanist ontology tends to strengthen a commitment to the privileging of vision and representationalism instanced by the insistence on the primacy of observation even when it is part of an otherwise idealist ontology as in the case of Ethnomethodology. By the same token, humanism's incorporation into a position that otherwise acknowledges visuality tends to weaken any impulse in a significatory direction and therefore any interest in invisible or non-human structures (as in the case of E.P. Thompson's Marxism).

Be such considerations as they may, I now wish to move on to outlining Jay's 'scopic regimes' in order to locate Postmodernism. According to Jay (1988), there were three such regimes within pre-modernist painting. The first is named after the technical advance in painting that made it possible, namely Alberti's invention of perspective in the fourteenth century. The difference that perspective made may be easily appreciated by contrasting any Pre-Renaissance painting (Http://www.artcyclopedia.com – search in 'Movements') with any Renaissance one (Http://www.artcyclopedia.com – search in 'Movements'). Jay calls this regime 'Cartesian perspectivalism' because he argues that the sense of distance that it produces also evokes the same coolness, objectivity and mastery that Descartes sought later as he moved towards formulating his *Cogito*. Thus he suggests that perspectivalism prefigured philosophical rationalism or idealism.

The second scopic regime Jay finds best exemplified in the domestic scenes common in early seventeenth-century Dutch painting (Http://www.artcyclopedia.com – 'Picture Search' for Jan Vermeer, *Woman Holding a Balance*). Following the art historian Svetlana Alpers (1983), he refers to this regime as the 'art of describing'. Of course perspective is deployed but in this case to get closer to the scene – to the objects, people, emotions and social life it represents. In this way, then, Jay argues that the 'art of describing' prefigured philosophical empiricism or positivism and may indeed have helped to bring it to realisation.

The third scopic regime is that instanced above all by late seventeenth-century Baroque painting (Http://www. artcyclo pedia.com – 'Picture Search' for Andrea Pozzo, *The Apotheosis of S. Ignazio*). Here the lessons drawn from perspectivalism and the 'art of describing' are combined with Kabbalistic and indeed Pythagorean ideas about the power of linguistic and mathematical representations (Yates, 1979, p. 25). The result is the production of an effect which is surrounding, enveloping and overwhelming, which produces in the viewer a sense of his or her subordination and helplessness in the face of a far greater power, namely God or a temporal absolute monarch. A similar sense of awe, bewilderment and individual finitude was also achieved in a more literary way through the use of classical allegories in other Baroque paintings. The philosophical position most closely correlated with rather than prefigured by such paintings was Leibniz's 'Monadology'. The reason why it was a correlate of rather than prefigured by the Baroque was because both were aspects of conscious social projects, namely the Counter-Reformation and rise of the absolute monarchies of Europe (Maravall, 1986). Thus, for example, a consequence of Leibniz's effort to reconcile rationalism with theism in his Monadology was his argument that one effect of our monadic or singular relation to the world was that we do not realise that we possess free will only in order to carry out God's will.

Although Jay does not do this, I will dare to suggest that these three scopic regimes may be schematically represented as follows:

RATIONALISM: *subjects* produce *representations* of *objects*
EMPIRICISM: *objects* evoke impressions in *subjects* who produce *representations*
THE BAROQUE: *representations* produce *objects* in the minds of *subjects*

As this schematicisation makes clear, if one substitutes the term 'representations' for that of 'symbols' in Figure 1 (see above, p. 8) it is clear that each of these visualities remains within the problematic of representationalism since the key elements have merely been rearranged rather than changed in any fundamental way.

POSTMODERNISM AS A BAROQUE VISUALITY

Before I specify the consequences of this for Postmodernism and indeed so that the analogy I wish to draw between developments in art and social theory will be easier to appreciate, I would like to take another chance and extend Jay's concept of scopic regimes to Modernist paintings. There are two reasons for this: first, it takes us closer to the style in which the postmodernists work; and second, the move in the direction of abstraction and self-conscious painterliness that appears to be intrinsic to Modern Art ironically makes the non-painterly components of the scopic regimes easier to recognise.

I will take John Constable (Http://www.artcyclopedia. com – 'Picture Search' for John Constable, *Flatford Mill (Scene on a Navigable River)* as exemplifying the ending of the separate development of the three regimes through his synthesis of the

concerns of all three as regards space, detail and affect. In order
that the difference made by what in my simple-minded sociological way I think of as the twin progenitors of the modernist
revolution in painting – the advance of natural-scientific knowledge and a newly assertive individualism – I would like the
reader to consider three modernist 'outdoor' scenes and compare them with Constable's and each other. The first is by
Cézanne (Http://www.artcyclopedia.com – 'Picture Search'
for Paul Cézanne, *Chestnut Trees at the Jas de Bouffan*) since one
can see in it evidence of both the Impressionist's knowledge of
Optics –the juxtapositioning of different colours to produce the
impression of others – and sense something of the painter's
emotional state from the coolness of the overall effect. The
second is by Pablo Picasso (Http://www.artcyclopedia.com –
'Picture Search' for Pablo Picasso, *House in a Garden*). This time
one can see evidence of the Cubist's knowledge of Optics in the
acknowledgement of the necessary fragmentariness of vision
that is the product of its saccadic character, as well as of – in
the virtuoso way in which he recombines the fragments – the
painter's joy at the possibilities that this acknowledgement
creates for individual expression. The third is by Salvador Dalí
(Http://www.artcyclopedia.com – 'Picture Search' for Salvador Dalí, *The Metamorphosis of Narcissus*). Here the science is in
the borrowing from Psychoanalysis evident in the nightmare
imagery, and both self-expression and a desire for affect in the
shock knowingly delivered to the viewer.

The first two paintings synthesise concerns with space and
description within the modernist register, while the third
synthesises these two concerns with one for affect while also
remaining in a modernist register. Now compare them with

a great postmodernist painting (Http://www.artcyclopedia. com – 'Picture Search' for R.B. Kitaj, *If not . . . not*). Its postmodernism is apparent above all in the eclecticism of the styles it incorporates and in the presence of multiple perspectives and none, as well as in its refusal to privilege any style or particular vanishing point. The effect is thus much more purely Baroque than Dalí's Surrealism in that we are made aware of an overwhelming force which reminds us of the pathos of our condition, albeit in this case the force is that which compels us to protest against tyranny – Kitaj's title is an abbreviated version of a Roman slogan which Charles Jencks (1986, p. 43) paraphrases as 'if you the king will not uphold our liberties, then we will not uphold you'. At this point it would also be appropriate to re-read Baudrillard's account of Disneyland (above, p. 138) which should now appear as clearly Baroque in its visuality if not its sensibility. Note, for example, not only the nature of his overall representation of Disneyland as a 'perfect model of all the entangled orders of simulation', but also his references to: the 'play of illusions and phantasms', the '*religious* revelling in real America', and the 'multitudinous affect' of 'warmth and affection' produced by an 'excessive number of gadgets'.

The significance of discovering that Postmodernism involves a repetition of the Baroque exaltation of vision (see also, Buci-Glucksmann, 1994) is not to confirm, say, Habermas's (1981) condemnation of it as inherently conservative in a political sense – indeed Kitaj's painting and Baudrillard's political sympathies suggest the opposite (see also, Pauline Rosenau's 1992 discussion of what she terms 'affirmative-postmodernism'). Rather, it is to show that it is deeply conservative or pre-Saussurian in its way of understanding the cultural sphere, since it is so convinced of the latter's power that it assumes that understanding it is a matter of simply decoding visible representations rather than of attending to the myriad invisible social and indeed other intellectual processes that produce such representations.

The questions that obviously arise are twofold. First, 'How could a body of thought that was initially made possible by the Saussurian revolution (see Baudrillard, 1981, for example) so comprehensively lose the plot?' Second, 'Is it possible to bring the Saussurian revolution to a conclusion that does finally free epistemology from representationalism?' It would be inappropriate to provide anything like a full answer to the first question here and besides a very comprehensive, painstaking but in my view unfortunately positive account has already been provided by Michele Barrett (1991). Barrett shows how poststructuralism was turned into an idealism, not in the sense of a non-materialism but in the more fundamental sense of a position that assumes that reality does not exist outside of language. Thus, incorporating my own corrective understandings, Lacan was read as privileging all signifiers over all signifieds without noticing that he was talking about the psychological unconscious only. Likewise, the later Barthes was read as always privileging connotation over denotation without noticing that he was talking about literature, and Derrida was read as privileging writing over speaking without noticing that his prey was a metaphysics of presence rather than scientific discourse as such. Finally, and perhaps most fatally Foucault was read as privileging discourse over all else. Because Foucault is the only one of these writers to speak directly of the social sciences, he has been the most egregiously misunderstood, and is the most pertinent to the possibility of the non-representationalist visuality that I seek, I will go to somewhat greater lengths to save him from the idealist reading that threatens to sideline him as a mere servant of the Baroque revival that was Postmodernism.

FOUCAULT AS A SOCIAL SCIENTIST

As I understand the trajectory of his thought, Foucault was always a social scientist and at the beginning and end of his career more specifically a psychologist rather than a philosopher. That is, the guiding thread of his studies was the founding of a psychology that was truly liberatory in that it was less concerned with 'normalising' troubled individuals than with returning them to a state of confidence and pleasure in themselves. For this reason, he focused his attention on the development of the 'normalising' disciplines such as psychiatry (Foucault, 1967) and medicine (Foucault, 1973). In the course of these studies he realised that the pathologising of individuals was a necessary prerequisite if they were to be normalised and that therefore scientific work involved the exercise of power in both its repressive and, as he was later to put it, 'productive' aspects. He then turned his attention to some of the other human sciences, specifically Linguistics, Political Economy and Natural History (Foucault, 1971), before stopping to take stock of and formalise the theoretical and methodological ideas that had somewhat inchoately informed his earlier studies. The title of this formalisation was *The Archaeology of Knowledge* (1972). In the Introduction to the *Archaeology*, he states that, inspired by Marx and

Nietzsche (ibid., pp. 11–14), what differentiated his approach to the archival evidence upon which he depended was that he had come to understand it as a set of 'monuments' rather than a set of 'documents'(ibid., pp. 6–7). That is, he had come to approach them by uncovering their surroundings in the manner of an archaeologist rather than by trying to imagine what kind of subjects in what kind of circumstances had given voice to them (for a more detailed accont of Foucault's development, see Pearce and Woodiwiss, 2001).

In Chapter 2 he introduces what to me are the critical concepts of the 'discursive formation' and the 'rules of formation of a discursive formation'. He begins by saying that, as he worked on the archives pertaining to medicine etc., he was continuously asking himself what gave them their unity or in other words what made them distinguishable as instances of particular knowledges. In trying to answer this question he considered four hypotheses. First, was it the objects that they were concerned with? Second, was it the 'style' or the particular way practitioners made statements about their objects of interest? Third, was it that the discourse was based upon a shared set of concepts? Or fourth, was it that the discourse exhibited a certain set of themes that underpinned and prompted conceptual development?

His conclusion was that each of these hypotheses on their own failed because of the heterogeneity apparent in the archival evidence:

Hence the idea of describing these dispersions themselves; of discovering whether between these elements, which are certainly not organised as a progressively deductive struc-ture, nor as an enormous book that is being gradually and continuously rewritten, nor as the oeuvre of a collective subject, one cannot discern a regularity: an order in their successive appearance, correlations in their simultaneity, assignable positions in a common space, a reciprocal functioning, linked and hierarchized transformations . . .

Whenever one can describe, between a number of statements, such a system of dispersion, whenever, between objects, types of statement, concepts, or thematic choices, one can define a regularity (an order, correlations, positions and functionings, transformations) we will say . . . that we are dealing with a *discursive formation* . . . . The conditions to which the elements of this division (objects, mode of statement, concepts, thematic choices) are subjected we shall call the '*rules of formation*'. The rules of formation are conditions of existence (but also of coexistence, maintenance, modification, and disappearance) in a given discursive division (Foucault, 1972, pp. 37–8, emphasis in the original).

Much of the remainder of the book is taken up with describing the rules of formation of the elements of the discursive formation. The rules with respect to 'objects' are: their 'surfaces of emergence' or the institutional sites where they appear; the 'authorities of delimitation' who predominate within these sites; and the 'grids of specification' such as the 'body', 'psyche' or 'soul' that the latter authorities use to demarcate their areas of expertise. The rules with respect to mode of statement or 'enunciative modalities' are: the identity of the qualified speakers; the institutional sites whence they speak; and the modes of 'interrogation' they take up (listening, questioning or looking, for example). The rules with respect to 'concepts' are:

their order and forms of succession; their fields and forms of coexistence; and the 'procedures for intervention' or working within the conceptual field as instanced by 'rewriting', 'transcribing' and 'translating'. Finally, the rules with respect to themes or 'strategies' are: the determination of their points of 'diffraction' and 'equivalence' or differentiation and systematisation; the identification of thematic authorities whether these are located within the field of discourse involved or external to it and are therefore authorities by analogy; and the identification of 'the *function* that the discourse under study must carry out *in a field of non-discursive practices*' (ibid., p. 68, emphasis in original), and '*possible positions of desire in relation to discourse*' (ibid., emphasis in original).

Having in this highly systematic way outlined his concepts and method and in so doing brought to the fore that imbrication of knowledge with power which is essential to reference and therefore constitutive of visuality – *vide* the centrality of various authorities throughout the rules of formation and the insistence on the functionality of discourses in the fields of non-discursive practices and desire – Foucault turned his attention to the other side of the discursive coin, so to speak, the power effects of discourse itself. These he investigated in *Discipline and Punish* (1977), and *The History of Sexuality*, vol. 1 (1979). In these 'genealogical' studies Foucault's focus is on developing his 'productive' concept of power as something that can make things happen for a wide variety of subjects instead of simply being repressive on behalf of a sovereign. However, it is important to be aware that this development is made possible by the concepts clarified in the *Archaeology* and in no way overturns them. Foucault may not use the archaeological language but when one considers the organisation and content of the two genealogical studies they are clearly structured in terms of the elements of the discursive formation and the rules of formation. In the final phase of his work, the latter two volumes of his *History of Sexuality*, Foucault returned to his quest for a liberatory psychology drawing on all he had learnt hitherto and sought to revive the ancient Greek idea of the 'care of the self' (Foucault, 1988 and 1990). Simultaneously, he also continued his study of power by developing his understanding of 'governmentality' or the *techne* of power (Burchell *et al.*, 1991).

It is clear, then, that Foucault is not a substantive idealist in the manner of the postmodernists in that he in no way privileges the discursive or cultural realm as that within which the remainder of sociality subsists. Discourse is self-evidently a realm of representations but it gains its socially determinative power not simply because of its representational character but because it is always part of variously constructed visualities, or as he put it 'regimes of truth', which are to be understood through the concepts of discursive formation and their rules of formation. That is, discourse gains its power as a result of a complex of imbricated representational and extra-discursive elements none of which are exhausted by their presence or role in particular discourses or even discursive formations but continue to subsist in many other forms and thus to be available for mobilisation within other discourses and discursive formations – how else would even discursive change be possible?

Equally clearly, and for many of the same reasons, Foucault is not a metatheoretical idealist either. Although he is clear that our knowledge of the world is always mediated through discourse, which is the point that has confused many of his readers, he is also clear that neither the world nor knowledge depends solely or even most importantly upon what is in our minds for its existence. On the contrary, as a rigorous materialist and non-humanist he very clearly conceptualises both as external to our minds, subsisting independently of them in the wider realm of an equally external sociality. Hence the necessity of hypothesising and ultimately modelling their structure as is clear from the way in which the concept of discursive formation was produced in the *Archaeology*. Hence also the testing of various hypotheses reported in the same place and carried out in his earlier substantive studies, as well as the testing of his model of discourse's structure, conditions of possibility and effects carried out in the genealogies. Hence, finally his respect for previous efforts to theorise the nature of the phenomena in which he was interested, whether they be those of, for example, Marx, Nietzsche, Saussure, Bataille, Behaviourist Psychology, Canguilhem, Merleau-Ponty or Althusser. All were valued because of their contribution to the imagining and substantive construction of an intellectual bridge across the gap that separates our minds from the things that we wish to understand.

In sum, although he never declared himself in these or any other metatheoretical terms – 'do not ask who I am' (Foucault, 1972, p. 17) – his work was premised upon a gradually emerging but in the end very sophisticated, non-humanist metatheory that has all the hallmarks of realism: an ontological insistence on the non-minded and material character of social reality that because of its ontological depth subsists as structures that, in terms of epistemology, cannot be observed spontaneously or directly but instead have to be modelled and tested before they can be spoken of with any and only ever a provisional confidence. And finally, because he took as his object of enquiry human knowledge itself, what he has bequeathed to us is not simply a series of substantive studies that have opened whole new areas of investigation but, most importantly in the present context, our most sophisticated current account of reference or, in other words, of how discourses and therefore the words they mobilise come to be taken (or not) as referring to certain separately subsisting things and actions in the world. Thus he completed, of course provisionally, the transformation in our understanding of language and the things that exist within it that Saussure initiated and which is pictured in Figure 1.

FOUCAULT AND THE (PROVISIONAL) COMPLETION OF THE SEMIOLOGICAL PROJECT

As is suggested by Figure 1, Lacan reconstructed our conception of the subject in the light of Saussure's significatory theory of language and so gave us some valuable insights into how it is that *parole* always contains more than *langue* denotatively allows; that is, because it is sometimes prompted by our language-like unconscious. Likewise, it seems to me that the other post-structuralists have provided us with sometimes more specifically sociological insights into the additional ways in which value or meaning is added in *parole*. The realm of *parole* is what Saussure termed the realm of external linguistics or of language in the world rather than in itself. As such it has to be approached from the outside in the search for additional determinations of its content and effects since these are not contained in *langue,* which it should not be forgotten refers only to the general conditions of existence of language not the actual entity itself or *langage*.

As Barthes (1972, p. 115) was perhaps the first to point out, in *parole* we are presented only with chains of signifiers (the material aspects of signs) not with their signifieds. The latter may therefore only be discovered by a process of decoding, of uncovering the initially invisible structures that call forth, so to speak, certain signifieds including but also exceeding those that are denotatively established in the pertinent lexicon (see the left-hand side of Figure 1). Thus decoding is not simply a matter of using a dictionary (if we grant for a moment that dictionaries are simply compendia of denotative meanings) but also of uncovering how connotations are added in the practical use of language as it is deployed in very variable contexts. Because value or meaning may only be added through the operation of the syntagmatic and paradigmatic relations that align certain signifiers and signifieds with one another, connotations may also only be added through the operation of additional structures that are syntagmatic and/or paradigmatic in nature.

Instances of additional syntagmatic structures were first uncovered by writers working within an approach similar to Saussurian linguistics if not directly influenced by it, namely Russian Formalism. Thus, with his study of the morphology of Russian folk tales, Vladimir Propp (1963) opened the way to the study of the genre and narrative structures that divide parole, discourse, stories, films or whatever into parts larger than a sentence, govern how these parts may be combined with one another and limit the combinations that are possible within a particular genre. Instances of additional paradigmatic structures were first uncovered by Marxist writers concerned with the study of ideologies which in a very simple sense may be understood as alternative lexicons – 'you say "market", I say "mode of production", let's call the whole thing off'. Such studies were brought firmly within the semiological orbit by Barthes and his conception of ideologies as myth-like structures and by Althusser and his elaboration of the process of 'interpellation' as the mode in which ideologies have their effects. This was the line of work that Foucault took to a new and transformative level of sophistication with his use of the neither idealist nor economistic conceptions of discursive formation and rules of formation in order to explain how those specialised lexicons (sets of paradigmatic associations) that we know as the disciplines are produced and have their effects, one of which is to ensure that dictionaries are permanently out of date. Thus Foucault completed the semiological analytical circle by suturing the gap between language and its wider social context that Saussure had opened (only temporarily in his own mind) when he insisted on the *sui generis* character of language.

Those who, often under the misread influence of Derrida, read Foucault as an idealist almost literally short-circuit the semiological analytical circle (see the truncated line marked *différance* in the lower left quarter of Figure 1). They typically do this for one or more of three reasons: 1) they simply misread *The Archaeology*; 2) they misread his later 'genealogical' texts as a rebuttal of his earlier 'archaeological' ones; 3) they misread the *Archaeology* as essentially a prolegomenon to a new theory of the subject. Instances of the first type of misreading occur when commentators either fail to see that the concept of discursive formation does not entitle one to treat all varieties of discourse as simply species of literature (Rorty, 1982, p. xiii), or confuse the concepts of discourse and discursive formation with one another (Laclau and Mouffe, 1985, p. 106; for a detailed crit-ique, see Woodiwiss, 1990a, pp. 64–71), or finally neglect and therefore miss the significance of Foucault's inclusion of 'sur-faces of emergence' (that is, institutional or social-structural sites) amongst the rules of formation of the objects of discursive formations (Bauman, 1992, pp. 69ff.).

Instances of the second type of misreading are too numer-ous to list, but they include all the commentary just mentioned. For within it genealogy is seen as the supposedly superior, dis-cursively focused mode of analysis that Foucault substitutes for archaeology instead of as the latter's re-focusing and continua-tion – that is, the use of the same categories to tell a story as Foucault sees it, including its productive as well as constraining power-effects, instead of to criticise those written by others and/or established in common sense. Instances of the third type of misreading are likewise very numerous and they typically occur among readers who see Foucault's contribution as pri-marily one of helping to resolve Althusser's problem with the articulation of subjects with ideology (Hall, 1997c).

The result is that, according to their own lights at least, the authors of these misreadings have not only to confuse the category of discourse with that of discursive formation and to see them both as mentalistic structures, but also to value the genealogies far more highly than the archaeologies. Whether or not, for example, discursive formations have any pertinence to the unconscious, Foucault is clear that they relate in the first instance to the conditions of possibility of discourse not to those of subjects. It is true, of course, that Foucault says, 'in seeking to define, outside all reference to a psychological or constituent subjectivity that may be involved in statements, archaeology touches on a question that is being posed today by psycho-analysis'. However, it is very unfortunate that in stressing this point certain readers ignore how the, to me, encouragingly long sentence continues:

[I]n trying to reveal the rules of formation of concepts, the modes of succession, connexion and coexistence of concepts, it touches on the problem of epistemological structures; in studying the formation of objects, the fields in which they emerge and are specified, in studying too the conditions of appropriation of discourses it touches on the analysis of social formations (Foucault, 1972, p. 207).

In sum, for one reason or another those who read Foucault as an idealist fail to see that, like the substantive studies out of which they emerged and which they later stimulated, the concepts of discursive formation and in particular the rules of formation are supposed to make two things clear. First, that the discursive realm is always imbricated with the non-discursive realm. And second, that therefore the process whereby specific discourses emerge and gain a certain autonomy as power–knowledge systems is a multi-dimensional social process and not a purely discursive one, even if one common result of this process is that the memory of the role of political and economic relations in it is suppressed.

VISUALITY AND METHODOLOGICAL RESPONSIBILITY

In the present context, however, the most significant failure of those who read Foucault as an idealist is their inability to acknowledge that he not only taught us how to understand the social production and effects of discourses but also how to better understand and therefore improve our practice as social scientists, as in other words the producers of discourse. Thus discursive formations and their rules of formation should be understood as not simply explaining how reference is achieved (or not) by particular discourses among whatever may be the pertinent segments of a population, but also as visualities. That is, they should also be understood as the conditions that allow us to see a particular field. Thus what Foucault has provided us with is a greatly enriched and much more profoundly sociological development of the commonplace idea that theories are to be understood as perspectives.

In other words, and so far from warranting an epistemological relativism, Foucault in fact provides what the Sociology of Knowledge from Karl Mannheim on has sought, namely both a way of understanding the social production of knowledge in a detailed fashion, and of making us aware of the complexity and limits of what we do when we theorise or indeed engage in any substantive social-scientific work. Thus, without going into any detail, it seems reasonable to me as a first approximation to explain the disciplinarily constitutive status of the classical authors with respect to Sociology's 'object' by reference to the dire social conditions obtaining in the interwar period and the fact that their possible return haunted sociologists as they sought to understand whether or not the post-1945 prosperity would hold and what the social consequences might be of either a positive or negative outcome. Robert Nisbet argues that the changes consequent on the revolutions of the eighteenth century so disrupted the hitherto prevailing sets of social relations in

Western Europe that previously invisible aspects of them suddenly became visible or 'problematised', to use Foucault's vocabulary. In a similar manner it seems to me that the disruptions attendant on the Great Depression had the same effect *vis-à-vis* certain aspects of what were by then overwhelmingly capitalist societies. More specifically, the principal institutional sites wherein the social was problematised were: 1) the capitalist economy (Could it be civilised?); 2) the state (Could it be reconstructed so that it was capable of managing any such civilising process?); 3) the sphere of public discourse (How might it be made to accommodate the task of civilising capitalism?); 4) class relations (Would the antagonisms they represented destroy capitalism or could they be managed?).[1] If this suggestion is even broadly correct, it is therefore more or less self-evident why the texts of Marx, Weber and Durkheim should be singled out from the welter of other nineteenth- and early twentieth-century sociological texts – theirs were quite simply the ones that spoke most cogently to these problems and, very importantly, their inter-relationships with one another.

Now, just as the privileging of the classical texts was a product of a complex set of changes within and tensions between the rules of formation of the discipline, then as the latter change and the tensions between them either relax, intensify or change their loci, so the component discourses or different schools within the discipline wax and wane in popularity and/or change in their foci. Neither any one of the elements of the discursive formation nor any of its rules of formation is ultimately determinant of the discursive outcomes. For example, sometimes the succession of concepts, etc. follows changes with respect to objects. Sometimes it does not, as in the case of Parsonian sociology's inability to theoretically acknowledge the particularity of the capitalist economy. Sometimes changes in objects are prompted by changes with respect to enunciative modalities. Sometimes they are not, as is instanced by the apparent decline of Postmodernism. Another way of referring to such changes and nonchanges, whatever their cause, is to say that the visuality changes or does not.

Thus, when we are engaged in theoretical work *per se* we cannot affect our inherited visuality through affecting the objects of the discursive formation unless, that is, we become authorities of delimitation and so capable of affecting the grid of specification that delimits our object of study and so defines its content. But even then the problematisation or not of issues is much more importantly determined by precisely the ongoing social developments that Sociology aspires to understand. An example of these possibilities and limits would be the rise of Feminism and feminists in the academy and the limits on their achievements imposed by the relatively unchanging nature of the other institutional sites in which women are located. Where of course we can have far greater direct affect on any inherited visuality is in the differences we can make to enunciative modalities, concepts and strategies (the appearance of every new theory demonstrates this). This, then, demarcates our area of freedom and responsibility. However, the extent of any effects of the exercise of any such freedom is again limited, this time because of the varying functionalities of particular discourses in the fields of non-discursive practices and desire. Examples of this would be, the decline in the perceived salience of Marxism not just in Sociology but in many other disciplines too following the collapse of the Soviet Union, and the rise of Queer Theory respectively.

Apart from enabling us to understand the differences we can make (and not make) to our inherited visualities, Foucault can also help us to understand how we should go about attempting to make whatever changes are within our capacity when we work on new theories or discourses. Here what we can learn directly from him is rather restricted because he did not claim to have provided either a sociology or a replacement for it. It is limited to a metatheoretical protocol which is a clarification of realist metatheory: namely, that our observations, data or evidence must be understood to be as much a product of a particular discursive formation and therefore of a visuality as our concepts. Thus not only do they too have to be considered as elements of the signified rather than of the referent but new or, better, rediscovered forms of evidence become possible (see above, p. 55). To use Bhaskar's term in the limited sense that I consider permissible, they too are therefore elements in the 'transitive' realm and as a result mentally dependent rather than elements in or of the mentally independent 'intransitive' realm. They are, then, like concepts in that they too are elements that are made to refer to the intransitive realm by the referential effects of the discursive formation. Thus the lessons that Foucault taught were the necessity of, as well as a method for, avoiding representationalism in the production of what, because of sociality's externality to our minds, must always be our representations of it. Unfortunately, this is not an easy lesson to learn because of our ingrained and in this case empiricist habits of mind.

The Postmodernists and indeed many others regard poststructuralism and Foucault in particular as justifying the view that all social theory can ever produce are varying and essentially arbitrary pictures of social reality, legitimated if at all by their ethical content (for a selection of such views, see Seidman, 1994; and for a critique of the equally ocularcentric variation on them contained within the supposedly Foucaultian 'govern-mentality' literature, see Woodiwiss, 1998, pp. 25–8). But I regard Foucault especially as providing us with the metatheore-tical basis for a new visuality beyond the classical, modern scopic regimes. This is a visuality that, although it may in the end always be beyond the ability of social scientists to control, provides us at last with a fully non-visually dependent but wholly socially and intellectually produced capacity to see beyond appearances and so possibly comprehend the inner structure of social relations in a far more sustained way than hitherto. And it might be that not only do the results prove to be as surprising as some of M.C. Escher's graphics (Http://www.artcyclopedia. com – 'Picture Search' for M.C. Escher, *Other World*), but also that developments in social science may at last come to prefigure those in art and so reverse the established relationship. At least, the current prominence of a Conceptual Art that sometimes takes the form of quoting chunks of social theory as well as pickling animals in the manner of Damien Hirst suggests that some artists think this is possible – suggestively, the artist Brian Catlin has termed some of his work, 'written sculpture' (Sinclair, 1997, p. 256).

CONCLUSION: SOCIOLOGY AS A DISCURSIVE FORMATION

I would like to conclude with a metaphor which I hope will neither over- nor under-represent (Woodiwiss, 1990a, pp. 33,

185–9) what has been argued above. As general phenomena and when regarded as visualities, discursive formations may be likened to the incredibly powerful and complex multimedia telescopes that astronomers currently use to explore the cosmos. That is, their component elements and their rules of formation may be likened to so many power sources. However, for these power sources to be effective they need to be focused through a succession of optical, auditory and other types of 'lenses'. In Sociology the equivalents of these 'lenses' are our theoretical discourses, and how we grind or otherwise prepare them for use is by developing them in empirical research. Because Sociology is an old science, certainly it is as old as many of the natural sciences, it has a huge variety of 'lenses' available. Unfortunately, many of them were not well made. Our difficulty is to decide which ones. Here, then, is where Foucault can help since thanks to him it is now possible to formulate a second rule of neo-classical method:

> *theoretical discourses that are wholly a product of a representa-tionalist theoretical practice should be discarded, while those that are not, or at least not entirely, the product of such a practice may be retained either as they are or for reworking.*

In sum and to continue with the metaphor of the telescope, the classical theorists contributed hugely to the discipline's four power sources in further defining its object, its mode of enun-ciation, its conceptual components and its broader theoretical strategies. Here, then, is also the reason why it is important not to elide the concepts of discourse and discursive formation with one another. That is, in order to appreciate properly the con-tribution of the classical theorists, it is important to distinguish their contributions at the level of the discipline as a whole from their elaborations of their own particular discourses. The latter may or may not be forgettable – this, rightly or wrongly, depends in part upon one's own metatheoretical commitments and substantive interests – but the former cannot be avoided even if they may still be forgotten since they have become productive conditions of the possibility of sociological work.

To my mind, then, what is sociologically and politically tragic about the conceptual displacement of capitalism by modernity is that the former's huge capacity, when unchecked, to generate poverty and inequality has all but disappeared from sociological view, despite Giddens' and Hall's recent declarations that this is not what they intended. If one believes these protestations of innocence, and I do, what the unintended deproblematisation of capitalism confirms is the heartless power of discursive formations and their rules. Regardless of one's intentions, some changes and/or misreadings of concepts mean that any resistance disappears that the preceding theoretical 'lens' may have offered relative to the most likely inhibiting balances (institutional, rhetorical and structural) obtaining with respect to the other elements of the discursive formation. Giddens argues at length and correctly that the achievements of social science are harder to appreciate than those of the natural sciences because when they are successful they become incorporated into the routines of social life and are therefore taken for granted (Giddens, 1984, pp. 348–54). However, what he does not acknowledge is that this incorporation can be for ill as well as for good.

Tragedy and irony are often related and perhaps the greatest irony in the story that was told in the previous chapter is that Giddens's and Hall's texts may now be read as delayed symptoms of the postmodernist moment which have given it an afterlife in theoretical and substantive sociology that it did not earn, so to speak, for itself. In Giddens' case, this is because he nostalgically became a Modernizationist some thirty years too late and in the wrong country (that is, in Britain instead of the United States). And in Hall's case, this is because he was apparently unable to resist taking up the terms modernity and postmodernity, presumably on the grounds that the sheer fact of their existence indicated that there were meanings around that had had to be named. In sum, what Giddens and Hall have inadvertently done is help the Postmodernists with that mirroring of the inside of our theoretical lenses that makes representation seem all-powerful.

CONCLUSION

Towards a Global Visuality

To write a conclusion to a text claiming to be a preface is a rather strange thing to do so I will do it in a strange way. That is, I will be less concerned to summarise what has gone before than to continue to develop my position. This said, I will begin the latter task by repeating the two rules of neo-classical sociological method and commenting on their significance for the possibility of creating a more truly universalistic social science than we currently have:

1   *It is a necessary but not a sufficient condition of non-representationalist theoretical development that it is undertaken in the context of substantive research.*
2   *Theoretical discourses that are wholly a product of a representationalist practice should be discarded, while those that are not, or at least not entirely, the product of such a practice may be retained either as they are or for reworking.*

These rules are minimal but decidedly exclusionary in their effect since they rule out not simply concepts with a manifestly representationalist provenance but also, most likely, all those that rest on empiricist, rationalist or humanist assumptions. What they exclude is therefore very clear. Consequently, it is not necessary for me to take up a position at the 'pearly gates' and decide which contributions should be allowed into the neo-classical heaven and which should not.

This said, let me now qualify the harshness of the exclusionary effect somewhat by repeating some of what was said in the Introduction concerning why the need for reworking arises. This is simply to say that it arises because of the inadequacy of our conception of social structure although, for reasons I will briefly indicate below, this conception is far less inadequate than we often think. Nevertheless, there is still a great deal of work to be done in recovering and reworking what we have already taught ourselves about social structure but have forgotten, let alone in discovering new things about its nature and interior. The reason we have forgotten so much is because, whether or not we have been mesmerised by *The Structure of Social Action*, we have tended to focus on 'social integration' and, unlike Lockwood, have seldom related it to 'system integration'. Thus much of what has been done is simply impertinent to the lack that has created the need for reworking. As a result, any judgement on its utility must logically wait on the arrival of an adequate conception of social structure – those positions whose proponents are not prepared to wait on this possibly still far-off event clearly rule themselves out of the neo-classical project, at least as I have conceived it, and no doubt much to their relief.

THE UNIVERSAL

So what, then, have we repressed that we once knew, or could have known, about social structure? The question can be answered surprisingly briefly because the answer is necessarily and pleasingly simple if rather abstract. It is necessarily simple and abstract because the fundamental concepts of a non-representationalist, neo-classical visuality and therefore the concept of social structure it makes possible must be very general as it is a condition of their utility that they lack any specific content. And this is despite their acceptability depending upon them having been produced in the course of substantive efforts to make sense of the social, as well as the fact that they gain new substantive content whenever they are re-used which may transform them. Thus, like the founders, we can cast aside our humble metaphors and say that social structure is the synthesis of what our concepts tell us is irreducible to and therefore constraining relative to 'human being and human doing'. That is, in our current state of knowledge and at the most general level, social structure is the sum of the interactive and mutually interpenetrative effects of economic, political and cultural or discursive positions – the last understood as sets of presences and absences with respect to how production in its narrowest sense is articulated with nature, and with respect to the non-discursive (political) and discursive modalities of discipline. Exemplifications of these sets of presences and absences in the case of a highly simplified model of the class structure in capitalist societies would be: possession/separation from the means of production; possession/separation from the means of controlling production; and possession/separation from legal title to the outcome of production.

As I have explained in considerable detail in a series of theoretical and substantive writings (see especially, Woodiwiss, 1990a, Ch. 9; and 1998, pp. 39–45), these presences and absences have *sui generis mutually determining effects* which are distinguishable from any that may be mediated through either human or non-human agents. Thus certain actions are either impossible or necessary (here is the constraint) along one or other of the different dimensions of sociality in so far as they are pertinent to class, given the interactive effects of these presences and absences. In the simplest case, I cannot require my employer to increase my salary and she or he cannot agree to my request simply because I need more money. This is not because, as Giddens would have it, the pertinent rules and resources are beyond either my own or my employer's grasp in time and space, but because, as a condition of their existence, they are necessarily beyond any human grasp. And this would be the case anywhere the salient sets of presences and absences obtained and irrespective of what must be their very varied local content (Woodiwiss, 1993, Chs 5 and 6; 1998, pp. 113–16, 157–60, 201–3, 229–30). In sum, then, because of the inter-active effects that constitute it, the capitalist class structure, like Lockwood's status order, simply is and agents may merely like it or lump it. The exception would be if they were able to tamper, and in the past at least this has been possible, with the sets of presences and absences in rather specific ways. However, even when this has been done, its possibility let alone any effective additional action can never be a matter of pure volition.

I have used the example of the class structure because this is the aspect, and let me emphasise that it is only one aspect, of social structure that has been most pertinent to my substantive interest in labour law and human rights. I have also used it because it is likely to confirm the worst fears of those who will be most strongly opposed to any sort of neo-classicism – it is simply a way of returning to the discredited ideas of a Structuralism defined by its insistence on the fixity of structures and a Marxism fixated on class. Anticipating such a response provides me with the opportunity to clarify further the nature of the neo-classical project as I conceive it.

Here the first point I wish to make is to reconfirm that the project does indeed involve a process of recovery but one of the entire classical repertoire of concepts not simply those associated with Structuralism and Marxism. The project is thus, in the first instance at least, an intervention designed to have an effect at the level of the discursive formation that is Sociology rather than with respect to the specific theorisations this may make possible. More specifically, concerning the fear of social and political passivity associated with any return of Structuralism, I will simply say that, as I hope is clear from the brief discussion of the class structure that was provided above, I took some care to point out that the approach I commend should enable one to distinguish more easily those actions that might bring about structural changes and those that cannot – for example, while asking for a salary increase will not ensure this happens, changing the law in various ways might do so.

Concerning the fear of what some have called 'class reductionism', I would like to say rather more because it is even more germane to the question of social structure. For me the three fundamental dimensions of sociality are neither exhausted, so to speak, within the class structure, nor are they to be confused with the institutions that we name after them – the economy, the polity and the cultural sphere. On the contrary, the three dimensions provide social structure with its depth for at least four reasons. First, they are all constitutive of each of the institutions we confusingly name after them and are therefore irreducible to any of them. Second, the sets of presences and absences that are possible in terms of them are in principle infinite, even if they are far more restricted in any specific social setting because of their mutual determination. Third and consequently, these sets are also constitutive – through either two-way, or internally differentiated one-way effects – of many other institutions and less clearly demarcated social entities. Examples would be religions and legal systems, or the discriminatory orders exemplified by racism (see Omi and Winant, 1994) and (hetero)sexism (see Gibson-Graham, 1996; Walby, 1990). Finally, they are also constitutive of the status orders that articulate all of these and much more together in terms of whatever may be the dominant public discourse. Fourth, all institutions and entities, in turn, both affect the nature of one another and produce the type of overall, syn-thetic effects that Marcel Mauss termed 'total social facts' (Woodiwiss, 1998, pp. 22–5).

In sum, then, social structure is a real, three-dimensional entity subsisting in the form of differently configurable and variously interactive sets of presences and absences with respect to how social life is organised economically, politically and cul-turally. Moreover, from whatever angle it is imagined or looked at, there are entities and processes that are closer or further away from its immediately perceptible surfaces – institutions are closer to the surface, while entities such as the class struc-ture are always further away. Thus we do indeed know more about the nature of social structure than we may have thought we did. The problem is that we know little more than its most basic parameters and certain limited regions of its interior. To improve our knowledge we need not only additional recovered but also new and differently focused concepts (see below, pp. 179ff), as well as new or, again, recovered methodologies. Thus, for example, what commends Foucaultian discourse analysis as a method is not just the status of discourse as genuine data (see above, p. 54) but also, as I have deployed it elsewhere (Woodiwiss, 1998, pp. 22–4, 49–50), its capacity to serve as an index or a way of investigating three-dimensional social relations *à la* Durkheim.

THE PROBLEM OF ORIENTALISM

This is all I wish to say by way of summary and self-commentary. Now I will turn to a consideration of what I am sure is only one of many challenges that neo-classicism will have to overcome if it is to deserve serious consideration as a strategy to advance Sociology's claim for that 'special competence' that Durkheim sought. This challenge is the orientalism (Said, 1979; Turner, 1978; 1994) of the classics. This I will take as symptomatic but in no way exhaustive of all Sociology's other cultural blindspots since it is the one that I most often have to struggle with myself. The existence of these blindspots is a serious challenge since, given the realism of my metatheoretical premises, I have claimed to descry in the classical theorists the core of a universalistic science whose most general concepts should be equally useful throughout the world. It is also a serious challenge because, for reasons that I will briefly summarise below, the classical theorists were manifestly orientalist not just in their marginal comments on and more substantial discussions of Asia but also in the way in which they defined the discipline. That is, to give a different twist to the argument between Connell and Collins (see above, pp. 22–8), Sociology as a discursive formation, as a system of power/knowledge was in part created by othering and/or denigrating 'Asia' as an object of study in order to bring the particularity of the 'West' into sharper focus.[1]

Thus Marx defined the specificity of Western capitalist societies by contrasting them not only to their feudal predecessors but also to those of Asia, via the concept of the 'Asiatic mode of production' or what Karl Wittfogel (1957) later termed 'oriental despotism'. Weber discovered the role of Protestantism in the rise of capitalism in the West not simply by contrasting it to Catholicism and Judaism but also by contrasting all three of them to Confucianism. Finally, less explicitly but unmistakeably nonetheless, Durkheim explained the relatively high level of the division of labour in the West by pointing to the more rapid weakening of the *conscience collective* in the West than in the East.

By these different means, then, the West was defined as more economically (Marx), politically (Weber) and morally (Durkheim) advanced than the East and therefore, silently, more worthy of study. As a result and at least until recently, Asian societies were studied either by anthropologists or within the problematic of development and therefore only as the potential sources of answers to questions about the causes of exoticism or backwardness. Most of the latter turned out to be supposedly cultural especially but not only – *vide* the Marxist stress on 'feudal' survivals – when the questions were posed by the Modernizationists. Hence, when 'development' did occur in East Asia, it not only had to be a 'miracle' in general terms but also because the secret ingredient was the very value system – Confucianism – that had hitherto been blamed for holding at least some parts of the continent back.

In sum, the challenge represented by the orientalism of the classics to any universalistic claims that might be made for a neo-classical social theory is very substantial. And it is not simply an abstractly conceived challenge since throughout Asia what might be termed 'indigenous' or, more critically, 'nativist' sociologies flourish – for example, there is an Islamic Sociology, and in Japan an influential school of thought committed to the idea that Japan is a unique society which is simply incomprehensible in Western sociological terms (Nakane, 1970; Murakami, 1984).

How, then, should this challenge be responded to? In three direct ways and one less direct way, I think. First and most obviously, by the continuation of the sociological work of Asian scholars. Second, given the realities of the distribution of sociological power, by the increased preparedness of Western scholars to read and publish Asian-produced materials. Third, through more work on and in each other's societies – I can personally vouch for this as an intellectually painful but effective means of beginning to cleanse one's concepts of any representationalist residues (see Woodiwiss, 1992, 1998, and especially the differences between them).

In Foucaultian terms, each of these three responses instance interventions at the level of the discursive formation in order to attempt to change the object of our discourse. It seems to me, moreover, that not only are all of them already occurring, but also that the successes (still too limited, of course) of feminist sociologists, for example, in achieving just such a change of object are most encouraging. However, as in the case of the feminist advance, there is always the possibility of a 'backlash'. As regards Asia, the occasion for this seems to have been provided by the recent financial crisis in that there has been a distinct suggestion of *schadenfreude* in many Western responses. My favourite, if that is the right word, example popped up quite unbidden but highlighted in Britain's otherwise impeccably politically correct *Guardian* newspaper in an article about the failure of a Hong Kong investment bank. Following up (?) on the fact that the bank had lost a lot of money in Indonesia, the article continued:

> But it is not merely a country that has melted down. Reckless growth, cronyism, corruption and secrecy have turned the region's economic miracle into a mirage and transformed the prophets of 'Asian values' into the architects of disaster. An entire philosophy has crumbled (Higgins, 1998).

The orientalism is as self-evident as the statement is ungrounded. This last because, as of the time of this writing, the greatest beneficiary of the crisis so far has been China, which is both a major proponent of the discourse of Asian values and has seen its wealth relative to much of the rest of Pacific Asia hugely increase when measured in United States dollars as other currencies have lost value and its own has remained stable. Maybe, then, the functionality of sociological discourse in relation to the non-discursive realm still favours interest in Asia – let us hope so.

TOWARDS A CONCEPT OF GLOBAL
SOCIAL STRUCTURE

Even if this should not prove to be the case, there is great promise in something that sociologists are doing that is not directly related to Asia but is nevertheless pertinent to the task of changing the object of our discursive formation. This is their reconceptualisation of the nature of sociality to take account of its inherently transnational character and so get to grips with what has become known as globalisation. The salience of this work to the problem of sociology's continuing parochialism is that it both very quickly exposes any Eurocentric, representationalist residues (Woodiwiss, 1996) and forces one to recognise the actual hybridity (Bhahba, 1994; Gilroy, 1994) of even local social relations. The challenge to our representational powers posed by globalisation may be best put in terms of a metaphor drawn by Edward Soja from the work of Jorge Luis Borges:

Then I saw the Aleph . . . . And here begins my despair as a writer . . . . In that single gigantic instant I saw millions of acts both delightful and awful; not one of them amazed me more than the fact that all of them occupied the same point in space without overlapping or transparency (Soja, 1989, p. 2).

This quotation summarises not only the criteria against which I think one should judge the success or otherwise of any efforts to meet the challenge represented by globalisation but also those against which the success or otherwise of a non-representationalist social science more generally should be judged. For this reason, then, I will specify what I think Borges might be saying to sociologists. For me the mythical creature, the Aleph, is a metaphor for the 'world as a single place', which is Roland Robertson's (1990) wonderfully concise definition of globality. For Borges, any writer's, including the sociological writer's, task is to produce a representation of the world that confronts him or her. And the reason that the Aleph (globality) evokes despair is because verbal representation is a necessarily linear process in that different sounds and graphic images cannot occupy the same time and/or space and remain intelligible, whereas the Aleph (globality) occupies 'the same point in space without overlapping or transparency'. The question that therefore has to be posed to all texts concerned with globalisation is: How well do they respond to the tension caused by the inadequacy of our means of representation?

At first sight visual, and therefore in epistemological terms representationalist, modes of representation would seem to be greatly advantaged over verbal or signifying modes with respect to representing the simultaneity of many different sorts and sets of social relations. Thus a painter can add emotion by his or her choice of lighting (light, dark, shadowed), medium (pencil, charcoal, watercolour, gouache, oil paint, etc.), mode of application (thin, thick, pointillist, soft- or hard-edged, etc.). He or she can also represent the simultaneity of social relations by introducing multiple perspectives, whether in the classical or cubist manner, and/or by resorting to collage, pastiche and eclecticism in the manner of the Kitaj painting referred to above (p. 145), and/or by setting up installations and performances. This said, vision-based modes of representation are unable to provide, as opposed to hint at, explanations for the presences or absences they represent, and it is therefore largely meaningless to check the accuracy of either their representations or their explanations.

By contrast, and to summarise the argument of this preface, conceptually produced representation and corrigible explanation are, or should be, the hallmarks of good social science. What both allows and requires such characteristics is precisely the fact that social science is something that subsists within language rather than within the visual domain. Thus social scientific modes of representation have at their disposal, or should have, methods of representation that because they should be significatory rather than representationalist, allow for and demand a much more complex response to the incommensurability that defines the relationship between the world and our means of representing it. Specifically, significatory modes of representation require us to define rigorously what is signified by our signifiers, to augment, enrich and transform our signifieds by observing in terms of the sign systems we construct, and to proffer explanations for the representations that the deployment of our sign systems produces by invoking the causal mechanisms that the same sign systems allow us to imagine. In this way, then, we can hope to represent simultaneity within an imagined multi-dimensional social world and so visualise 'millions of acts both delightful and awful . . . [which occupy] the same point in space without overlapping or transparency'.

Thus, although David Held and his co-authors (1999) have recently provided us with a comprehensive and superbly detailed description of the four systems of 'interconnections' (political, military, economic and cultural) that comprise contemporary globality, there is a need to go further, much further.

For theirs is a Giddensian and therefore an explicitly if not self-consciously representationalist project in that their concern is to specify the visible 'extensity', 'intensity' and 'velocity' of the globalising forces in order to delineate the 'shape' of contemporary globalisation. It therefore stops short of investigating the imbrication and interpenetration of these forces and so specifying the *sui generis*, inner structure of globality that makes it a social entity that is far more than the sum of its parts. Unfortunately, one result is that their study is marred by unconscious but pervasive Ameri and Euro-centrisms which arise because of the manifestly Western provenance and leadership of most of the institutions and organisations upon which they focus. However, if one concerns oneself instead with more strictly social entities and the forces that both constitute and arise from them, a rather different picture is produced. This is one in which institutions, organisations and indeed their policies and leaders are the product of what might be termed 'subterranean' or 'geological' local as well as transnational forces which are by no means entirely, even if the latter are currently predominantly, Western in their character or provenance. It is therefore a picture which socially rather than simply politically problematises the current Western dominance (compare, for example, the discussion of human rights in Held *et al.* (ibid.) with that in Woodiwiss, 1998, 2000).

What, then, might the inner structure of globality look like? If Held *et al.*, as well as the many other writers about globalisation – the majority – whose work they have brought to some kind of climax, fail what might be termed the 'Aleph Test' because they emphasise the transnational at the expense of the national or the local, then the principal critics of their line of reasoning, Paul Hirst and Grahame Thompson (1999), fail the same test because they stress the national at the expense of the transnational (Woodiwiss, 1996). In sum, both of the main schools of thought concerning globalisation conceptualise it as an either/or problem according to which either transnational forces are sweeping all before them or they are not because of the inherent stength of the nation state; that is, in both cases the international is rendered epiphenomenal and so denied any intrinsic effects of its own. By contrast, for me globalisation is best problematised as a possibly emergent property of the intensification of international relations that is a product of the increased tensions between transnational and local forces. Thus it may be most usefully approached as a relational phenomenon in that it is a matter of necessarily interactive effects in motion rather than a matter of interactions between the macro and the micro and/or the dynamic and the static. The result is that, whereas much of the literature has, dominated by the figure of 'imperialism', misread Robertson's definition of globalisation as an argument that the world is becoming increasingly the same place, I wish to insist that we investigate the nature of its possibly increasing singularity. Interestingly, both sets of proponents of the either/or analytic remain in the thrall of the cartographical and therefore representationalist image of the world as a collection of nation states. The believers in globalisation tend to figure it as an emerging, Western or American-dominated superstate while their critics tend to ground their scepticism in their conviction that no such entity is conceivable.

Thus, if one wishes to perceive the nature of global singularity, and given the a-priori implausibility and mutual exclusivity of the extant positions, it is therefore essential to be clear that any possibly emergent, single global place can only exist within social as opposed to geographical space. Consequently, when seeking evidence of the emergence of a single global place one does not have to demonstrate the ongoing collapse of all national boundaries and the disappearance of all differences since this would only be necessary if one were seeking evidence for the emergence of a single, state-like entity. Rather, without denying the current Western or American predominance, one simply has to demonstrate that a distinguishable global dimension of social life has emerged which has effects throughout the world and to which states and indeed international organisations themselves have had to respond. In other words, just as Durkheim argued that we know that there is a dimension of social life that is not reducible to the interactions between individuals because individuals are not free, and do not even feel free, to do exactly as they please even when they are on their own, so we can say that globality exists as a social fact insofar as we can demonstrate that states and international organisations, whether public or private, are likewise not always free to do as they please.

Apart from changing the focus of studies of globalisation, the problematisation of it as a phenomenon of the international realm and a matter of singularity rather than sameness, also simplifies the issue of dating its appearance. This is because one is no longer looking, like Held *et al.* (1999, p. 16), for evidence of a process of huge vagueness and generality – to wit 'a process . . . which embodies a transformation . . . [of] . . . transcontinental or interregional flows' – but something much more specific. As what I imagine to be Held *et al.*'s exhaustion at the end of their labours may have told them, they had embarked on an impossible task – how to compress the history of the world into a few chapters. That way madness lies, as is attested by the apparently barking scholar my brother met in the Library of Congress one day who had set himself the task of summarising the history of the world in a single sentence but by the time of their meeting had only managed to get in down to five pages!

Approached as an emergent property of the international system, the task of roughly dating the onset of globalisation becomes much less maddening since the state system itself is barely 350 years old and international organisations first appeared only a hundred or so years ago. In order to establish the existence of a variety of social constraint that is ascribable to globalisation, one therefore has to do just three things. First, examine the development of international political, economic and cultural institutions over the past one hundred years or so, asking the question 'What problems were/are they responses to?' Second, determine whether or not these problems have a content that may be identified as supranational in any way. This is because in specifying any such content and the institutions within which it is problematised one will be beginning to specify the nature of global social life. Third, show how any global social relations so discovered constrain, affect or, better, constitute national or local social life.

Concerning the first of these tasks, it is widely known that international governmental (IGOs) and international non-governmental organisations (INGOs) have grow enormously over the past 100 or so years: whereas there were less than 50 IGOs in 1890 and the first INGOs did not appear until until the early years of the last century, today there are more than

300 IGOs and around 4,500 INGOs (Willetts, 1997). More-over and moving on to the second task, we also know, thanks to Craig Murphy's (1994) essential work, that IGOs emerged in response to a particular set of problems whose solutions were remarkably quickly recognised as requiring efforts that were be-yond the capabilities of nation states even during so nationalistic a period. Thus in 1914, the year that the First World War broke out, 33 IGOs already existed which recognised that, to use Murphy's categories, 'fostering industry', 'managing potential social conflicts', 'strengthening states and the state system', and 'strengthening society' were each problems requiring interna-tional co-operation for their solution. Today, the same four problems continue to require such co-operation and since the 1970s they have been joined by environmental issues (see also, Waters, 1995, chs 4 and 5). These five sets of problems, then, have been defined by at least a plurality of governments as having dimensions that are supranational in their scope and significance and therefore beyond the capacities of nation states to solve. They not only have given rise to an increasingly dense and intense set of international social relations that have been described very well by Held *et al.* (1999, pp. 55–57) but they also therefore comprise the content of a distinctively global dimension of social life. The latter has been made visible by the changing forms of international governmental organisations in that, where once they were clearly subordinate to their member states, they now aspire to be, and in some instances actually are (*vide* the World Trade Organisation [WTO]), superordinate in relation to them.

The fact that many of the problems that give global social life a content that compels the attention of nation states to the degree that they have been prepared to forgo a certain quantum of their sovereignty have economic roots may, of course, be explained by the capitalist form taken by much economic activity over the past two hundred or so years. That is, economic forces have been pre-eminent in driving the formation of a global social space because the profit-seeking dynamic that is basic to capitalism implies the geographical extension of activities insofar as such extension promises either cheaper inputs or larger markets for outputs. However, global economic integration, whether with respect to trade, finance or the activities of large corporations, is precisely what Hirst and Thompson argue has not occurred. Despite the fact that even if Hirst and Thompson were correct one could still make a case for globalisation since the problems identified by Murphy as spawning a global social space are not restricted to the economic realm and where they are economic are not exhausted by Hirst and Thompson's triumvirate (i.e. they include issues relating to communications of all kinds, industrial standards, intellectual as well as other property rights, and labour), it is nevertheless useful to counter their scepticism since, ironically, it strengthens the case for the reality of globalisation still more.

Hirst and Thompson do not dispute the claim that the present level of international trade indicates a high level of economic integration but rather the idea that it is unprecedented. They point out that in proportionate terms current levels of, and national degrees of involvement in, world trade had been achieved prior to 1914 under the British-sponsored free trade regime. Thus their reading of the current trade situation is that it represents the restoration of a pre-existing condition not the arrival of a new one. However, their argument loses much of its plausibility once one does three things. First, takes account of the absolute numbers involved today, both in volume and value terms, since their hugely greater size means that the local impact of trade is far more consequential in terms of the range of products traded, degrees of market penetration and associated lifestyle and other social changes than it was in the nineteenth century. Second, considers the extent of trading networks today, which again are far wider and more intense than they were in the nineteenth century (Held *et al.*, 1999, pp. 165ff.). Third, notes that trade is now governed by a specifically global body, the WTO, which is far more inclusive than the British-dominated, free trade system. The WTO admittedly consists of national delegates and is dominated by the American-led G7 countries, but as the lack of progress on the G7's agenda at both the Singapore (1996) and Seattle (1999) meetings testifies the latter cannot always assume that they will get their way.

As regards finance, Hirst and Thompson also argue for the restoration of nineteenth-century conditions rather than the arrival of a new condition. In this case this is primarily because national levels of investment remain equally closely correlated with national levels of saving and therefore have been little affected by the huge sums of capital supposedly sloshing around within the global financial system. However, again both the volumes involved and the facts that most foreign investment now comes from private rather than governmental or international sources and much of it takes the form of stocks, bonds and derivatives thereof rather than bricks, mortar and machinery means that, especially given the new means of electronic communication, it is far more mobile than it was.

The consequence is that short-term movements can have a far greater impact over a far larger area than in the past as the recent 'Asian Crisis' made so clear.

Finally, with regard to the supposed role of large corporations in the integration of world economy, Hirst and Thompson (1999, pp. 94–5) argue that between 65 and 70 per cent of their value added arises from home territory activities and that therefore two things follow. First, large corporations are at most multinational enterprises and very seldom truely transnational ones. And second, such corporations represent neither the huge drains with respect to their home economies nor the Trojan horses with respect to overseas economies that the proponents of globalisation see them as. However, Hirst and Thompson's chosen measures once again make it hard for them to perceive the increased salience of the transnational dimension since they privilege ownership relations at the expense of marketing and production relations in their account of large corporations. Since much of the latter types of activity is carried out by legally independent sub-contractors, Hirst and Thompson therefore hugely underestimate the size of the capital base upon which what might be best termed today's 'virtual corporations' operate (Dicken, 1998). More specifically, since up to 75 per cent of total investment in international production is raised from local and other sources external to large corporations (Held *et al.*, 1999, p. 237), Hirst and Thompson's figures with respect to the home and overseas components of value added are either largely meaningless or simply beside the point.

In sum, then, although Hirst and Thompson are quite correct to insist that we certainly do not live in the 'borderless world' imagined by such globalisation enthusiasts as Ohmae (1990),

they are mistaken in denying that there is any evidence of movement in this direction with respect to their areas of interest.
They are, moreover, equally wrong in the corollary they derive
from their economic argument, namely that if globalisation is
not happening at the economic level, it is not happening
politically or culturally either (Hirst and Thompson, 1999,
p. 3). Not only is this argument intrinsically suspect because of
its surprising economic essentialism, but it is also empirically
suspect as I have already suggested with respect to political relations and will shortly suggest with respect to cultural relations.

Thus far I have argued that the emerging global social space
is essentially characterised by its singularity rather than any
Western or American-defined sameness. That is, it is instead
best conceived of as a response to a set of sometimes interlinked
problems in the political sphere which states have felt unable to
deal with individually, and which in the economic sphere
private institutions have felt unable to deal with inside the
boundaries of a single nation states. Both types of institutions
have therefore felt compelled to respond by creating an ever
denser network of increasingly autonomous and again sometimes interlinked global political and private economic institutions or networks which have steadily gained the capacity to
discipline even the most powerful states and corporations.

Further support for this position may be adduced by
considering the ongoing debate concerning the nature of the
global cultural sphere. One party to this debate have been those
who, taking their lead from such as C.L.R. James and Franz
Fanon and privileging the transnational over the national and
local, see our present and especially the future global culture as
largely the product of Western and more specifically American

cultural imperialism (see, for example, Schiller, 1970, Sklair, 1991, and Bourdieu and Wacquant, 1999). The other, and to me more convincing, party to the debate has comprised those who, again without denying the current strength of Western cultural influences, have adopted a post-colonial stance and stressed the resistant or, better, positive capacities of national and local cultures (Ang, 1996; Buell, 1994; Bhabha, 1994; Featherstone, 1995; Jameson and Miyoshi, 1998; Tomlinson, 1999). The result has been an argument for both the hybrid character of global culture and the irresistibility of the hybridisation process whether one is talking about northern or southern cultures, and also therefore an argument for singularity rather than sameness as evidence for the existence of a global cultural realm.

The foregoing, then, establishes in outline the social fact of globalisation in a Durkheimian manner. That is, its *sui generis* social reality has been established by describing its exterior morphological form in that the institutions and networks that have been referred to have interacted with one another to, in the language of the quotation from Durkheim used earlier (see above p. 55), disengage what is quite literally a whole world of diverse economic, political and cultural elements 'which, once born, obey laws of their own [and] . . . attract each other, repel each other, unite, divide themselves and multiply, though these combinations are not commanded and necessitated by the condition of the underlying [local] reality'. I would now like to move on to my third task and both suggest how global social relations affect or constitute national or local social life and, in so doing, say something about the physiology or inner structure of the global social fact.

For reasons that I have explained at length elsewhere
(Woodiwiss, 1998, ch. 1), those who have done most to make it
possible for us to understand the inner structure of globality
that Held *et al.*, as well as all those writers about globalisation,
the majority, whom they represent, ignore are Michael Mann
(1986), Bob Jessop (1990), Fred Halliday (1994), and David
Ruccio *et al.* (1991). Pleasingly, all of them have excellent neo-
classical credentials and for now it is sufficient merely to list
summarily our debts to them: to Mann we owe the insight as to
the inherently and inexhaustibly transnational nature of social
relations; to Jessop we owe the insight as to the sociological
nature of the state and the consequent multiplicity of its
interfaces with its national, international and transnational
environments; to Halliday we owe the insight as to the extreme
porosity of national boundaries that is apparent once one
combines Mann's and Jessop's insights; and to Ruccio *et al.* we
owe the insight that this porosity applies equally to the relations
that are constitutive of the class structure.

Since, although they arrived at their position independently,
Ruccio *et al.*'s insight is both a *terminus ad quem* of this chain of
insights and the one which is most directly pertinent to the
present argument, it provides the best point at which to begin
an outline of what is, I again emphasise in this context, but one
region of globality's inner structure, namely that pertaining to
the class structure. At this point it is important to remind
oneself of Durkheim's refusal of functionalism and therefore
teleology by being clear that utility is never a sufficient cause for
the appearance of social facts. Nevertheless, in order to establish
the general pertinence of globalisation for class relations, it is
valid to repeat the point made earlier concerning the centrality

of capitalism and the social conflicts it engenders amongst the problems that stimulated the rise of, first, the international and, latterly, the global institutions that have subsequently made globalisation into a social fact. Why this should be the case is made very clear by the 1918 preamble to the constitution of one of the first global institutions, the International Labour Organisation (ILO):

Whereas universal and lasting peace can be established only if it is based upon social justice;

And whereas conditions of labour exist involving such injustice, hardship and privation to large numbers of people as to produce unrest so great that the peace and harmony of the world are imperilled; and an improvement in those conditions is urgently required; as, for example, by the regulation of the hours of work, including the establishment of the maximum working day and week, the regulation of the labour supply, the prevention of unemployment, the provision of an adequate living wage, the protection of the worker against sickness, disease and injury arising out of his employment, the protection of children, young persons and women, provision for old age and injury, protection of the interests of workers when employed in countries other than their own, recognition of the principle of equal remuneration for work of equal value, recognition of the principle of freedom of association, the organisation of vocational and technical education and other measures;

Whereas also the failure of any nation to adopt humane conditions of labour is an obstacle in the way of other nations which desire to improve the conditions in their own countries.

What this text makes clear is, first, that to the states which formed the ILO class relations were intrinsically global in that, according to the second paragraph, either they might spiral out of control and eventuate in the sort of military conflicts that had so recently traumatised so many of them, or, according to the third paragraph, they might initiate just that 'race to the bottom' that many currently fear may be the result of globalisation. What the preamble also makes clear in the list of possible palliative measures that it includes is how exactly the ILO as a global institution might affect local class relations. The significance of this list is made still clearer if it is read in conjunction with the following extract from one of my own books:

a) the law may alter the balance with respect to the economic *possession* of the means of production to labour's advantage by granting certain 'liberties' to bargain over the terms of employment and/or by inscribing certain 'claims' within the conditions governing the hiring of labour and therefore the validity of the employment contract. These are generally referred to as 'labour standards' and include rules governing the payment of wages, rest periods and holidays. However they also include such aspects of collective labour law as those pertaining to the permissibility or otherwise of the closed shop. The inscription of such 'liberties' and/or 'claims' may or may not be accompanied by the granting to labour of participative 'powers' of one kind or another with respect to the setting of such standards.

b) the law may alter the balance with respect to political or
disciplinary *control* of the means of production to labour's
advantage in three ways; first, by granting certain
'liberties' to bargain over the conditions of employment
and/or by inscribing either certain 'claims' within the
employment contract in the form of those aspects of
'labour standards' that refer to workplace rules; second,
by limiting the contract's purview through specifying
certain additional 'liberties' which may allow its temporary suspension for bargaining purposes; third, by specifying in either workplace rules and/or the employment
contract certain 'claims' that allow for the exercise of
'powers' of one kind or another which allow varying
degrees of co-determination as well as the adjudication
of disputes by tripartite tribunals or mutually agreed
third parties.

c) the law may alter the balance with respect to *title* to the
means of production to labour's advantage by granting
certain liberties to bargain over ownership and/or by
inscribing various 'claims' within property, company and
taxation law in order to achieve such as profit-sharing,
employee share-ownership, nationalisation, and/or dis-
tribute social benefits of one kind or another. Again, the
inscription of such claims may or may not be accompanied
by the granting of certain participative 'powers' to labour
at the enterprise and/or national levels (Woodiwiss,
1998, pp. 49–50).

To those who read the possibility of such developments and in
particular their reversal over the past twenty years within the

problematic of imperialism and sameness, they are evidence for the emergence of a global ruling class which lords it with increasing impunity over an equally global proletariat (Pettman, 1979, p. 154; Sklair, 1991). However, such a reading involves a privileging of the transnational over the national that rather precisely obscures the nature of globality's inner structure. I say this because it fails to acknowledge what Mann (1993) and Carolyn Vogler (1985) among others have made so clear, namely that class relations are inevitably, if no longer solely, played out within nation states. Moreover, it has been rendered anachronistic by Ruccio *et al.*'s insight to the effect that the transnational, international and national dimensions of class are necessarily fused with one another in that they are the conditions for each other's existence.

The significance of this reciprocal conditioning may be brought out by considering some elements of the background to the recent WTO debate over a Social Clause. First, whereas British trade unions adopted a very nationalist posture durng the 1970s when they felt domestically politically powerful, they became increasingly pro-European and, at least in this sense, internationalist as their domestic power was eroded following Mrs Thatcher's election in 1979. Second, the American trade union federation, the AFL-CIO, became increasingly nationalistic and protectionist as its already minimal domestic power was still further eroded under the Reagan and Bush Administrations over the same period. Thus two major Northern trade union federations deployed very different rhetorics in favour of the incorporation of a Social Clause into the protocols of the WTO which would require the acknowledgment of certain basic labour rights as a condition of national participation in any further liberalisation of world trade. Third, most segments of capital in the South and the emerging economies of Pacific Asia became much more sceptical of globalisation as domestic pressure from trade unionists and other citizen groups forced their Northern counterparts to place the Social Clause on the WTO agenda. The political result was the spectacular impasse apparent at the Seattle Meeting of 1999. The analytical lessons to be drawn from even so crudely sketched a conjuncture are at least threefold. First, economically determined class unity is at least as unlikely at the global level as it has long been shown to be at the national level. Second, any even putative global state is at least as unlikely to be a unified 'executive committee of the bourgeoisie' as it long been shown to be at the national level. Third, and most generally, the fusing of the transnational, international and national dimensions of the class structure that is a consequence of globalisation is as likely to lead to the reproduction of national difference and indeed global chaos as it is to lead to sameness and unity. All this is because, to repeat one last time the quotation from Durkheim used earlier, globalisation has indeed disengaged a set of processes that 'obey laws of their own . . . [which are] . . . are not commanded and necessitated by the condition of the underlying [local] reality'.

In sum, then, the inner structure of globality inheres in the presently unavoidable articulation of transnational, international and national sets of social relations and, within the region of class relations at least, the differences this articulation makes to the presences and absences or balances between the classes as regards their possession/separation from the means of production, their political and cultural standing, and therefore the calculations made by those who claim to represent them.

Finally, the significance of grasping the inner structure of globality does not reside solely in what it tells us about the advisedness or otherwise of taking up one position or another within a somewhat arcane debate concerning the merits of a non-representationalist as opposed to a representationalist approach to constructing social theory. For it has substantive political significance too. This is because it implies that the possibility of just global governance does not rest on the creation of a unitary value system, even one so admirable to many Western minds, including mine, as the 'individual autonomy' commended by Held (1997, p. 271), or indeed on the establishment of a more general, unitary and state-like structure. Rather it depends on finding ways in which divergent values may be translated into each other's terms. And this, in turn, means discovering structures, or probably more accurately procedures, that allow both for the negotiation of difference and value enforcement in what will remain a very diverse set of global social circumstances.

These, then, are some of my reasons for thinking that there may yet come a time when social theory's current blind-spots have been overcome and its claim to universality for its 'special competence' may command global assent. And my hope is that it will come sooner rather than later since there is important work (Woodiwiss, forthcoming) that only sociologists can do in the area of human rights enforcement.

Notes

1   From Vision to Visuality in Classical Social Theory
1   My knowledge of eighteenth- and nineteenth-century Linguistics is largely derived from Foucault, 1971 and Seuren, 1998.

3   Myopia and Modernity
1   Compare the rapid increase in the number of index references to 'modernity' with the equally rapid decline in the number of such references to 'capitalism' in any book on social theory after, say, 1985. Also, note that even books by or on the supposedly Simmel-inspired Critical Theorists contained few if any references to 'modernity' before the same date.
2   As the late and recently demonised Louis Althusser (1994, p. 223) pointed out with a nice touch of irony:

> the craziest ideas based on the most implausible eclecticism and feeble-minded theory are in fashion, under the pretext of so-called 'post-modernism', in which, yet again, 'matter has disappeared', giving way to the 'immateriality' of communication (the latest theoretical concoction which not surprisingly justifies itself on the basis of the impressive evidence of the new technology).

3   For equally strong traces of Social Modernism in Giddens's political discourse, see his 1994b and 1998 texts where his discussions of 'positive welfare', 'active trust', and 'generative politics' carry clear validations of, in turn, self-reliance, responsibility and loyalty, and opportunity. What makes Giddens's position closer to a Clintonite or 'communitarian' version of Social Modernism (that is, an attempted synthesis of the Democratic stress on opportunity

196

and the Republican stress on self-reliance) in contrast to Bauman's 1950s' version, is the former's clearer conviction that even these values have yet to be fully realised – as Giddens (1994a, p. 35) says (apologetically?) '[we are dealing with] what after all remains a class society'. Also, corroboratively, he adds to his list of desiderata the two principal demands of the American New Left in the 1960s, participatory democracy and peace.

4   On Giddens' utopianism, see Perry Anderson's (1994, p. 43) comments on Giddens' earlier political pronouncements. It seems that one now needs an appreciation of ontological stratification both to realise that politically 'you can't make an omelette without cracking eggs'. All of which prompts critical thoughts about the policy prescriptions of the self-declared 'modernisers' of the British Labour Party. But thereby hangs another (how closely related?) tale (for the beginnings of such a tale see Elliot, 1999, and Neocleous 1999).

4   *Visuality after Postmodernism*
1   For my own understandings of how these problematisations occurred and their very different resolutions in the United States and Japan, see Woodiwiss, 1990b and 1992).

Conclusion   Towards a Global Visuality
1   I have placed the terms Asia and the West in 'scare quotes' because I recognise the stereotyping that they instance. However, I will not use the quotation marks in what follows in order to acknowledge that, regrettably, we still have not overcome these stereotypes.

References

Abrams, P. (1968) *The Origins of British Sociology*, 1834–1914, Chicago, University of Chicago Press.

Alexander, J. (1982) *Theoretical Logic in Sociology: Positivism, Presuppositions and Currrent Controversies*, London, Routledge & Kegan Paul.

Alexander, J. (1987) 'The centrality of the Classics' in Giddens and Turner (1987).

Alexander, J. (1995) Fin de Siècle *Social Theory: Relativism, Reduction and the Problem of Reason*, London, Verso.

Alpers, S. (1983) *The Art of Describing: Dutch Art in the Seventeenth Century*, Chicago, University of Chicago Press.

Althusser, L. (1969) *For Marx*, London, Allen Lane.

Althusser, L. (1994) *The Future Lasts a Long Time*, London, Vintage.

Anderson, P. (1992) *English Questions*, London, Verso.

Anderson, P. (1994) 'Power, politics and the enlightenment', in Miliband (1994).

Ang, I. (1996) *Living Room Wars: Rethinking Media Audiences for a Postmodern World*, London, Routledge.

Barrett, M. (1991) *The Politics of Truth*, Cambridge, Polity.

Barthes, R. (1972) *Mythologies*, London, Cape.

Baudrillard, J. (1981) *For a Critique of the Political Economy of the Sign*, St. Louis, Kansas, Telos Press.

Bauman, Z. (1987) *Legislators and Interpreters: On Modernity, Post-modernity and Intellectuals*, Ithaca, NY, Cornell University Press.

Bauman, Z. (1992) *Intimations of Postmodernity*, London, Routledge.

Baylis, J. and Smith, S. (1997) *The Globalisation of World Politics*, Oxford, Oxford University Press.

Bell, D. (1960) *The End of Ideology*, Cambridge, MA, Harvard University Press.

Bell, D. (1967) *Marxian Socialism in the United States*, Princeton, NJ, Princeton University Press.

Bell, D. (1973) *The Coming of Post-Industrial Society*, New York, Basic Books.

Bell, D. (1976) *The Cultural Contradictions of Capitalism*, New York, Basic Books.

Benton, E. (1977) *The Philosophical Foundations of the Three Sociologies*, London, Routledge.

Berman, M. (1982) *All That's Solid Melts Into Air*, London, Verso.

Bernstein, R. (ed.) (1985) *Habermas and Modernity*, Cambridge, Polity.

Bhabha, H. (1994) *The Location of Culture*, London, Routledge.

Bhaskar, R. (1978) *A Realist Theory of Science*, Brighton, Harvester.

Bhaskar, R. (1989), *Reclaiming Reality*, London, Verso.

Bourdieu, P. and Wacquant, L. (1999) 'On the cunning of imperialist reason', *Theory, Culture and Society*, vol. 16, no. 1, pp. 41–58.

Boyd, R., Gaspar, P. and Trout, J.D. (eds) (1991) *The Philosophy of Science*, Cambridge, MA, MIT Press.

Braidotti, R. (1991) *Patterns of Dissonance*, London, Routledge.

Brick, H. (1986) *Daniel Bell and the Decline of Intellectual Radicalism: Social Theory and Political Reconciliation in the 1940s*, Madison, University of Wisconsin Press.

Buci-Glucksmann, C. (1994) *Baroque Reason*, London, Sage.

Buck-Morse, S. (1991) *The Dialectic of Seeing: Walter Benjamin and the Arcades Project*, Cambridge, MA, MIT Press.

Buell, F. (1994) *National Culture and the Global System*, Baltimore, MD, The Johns Hopkins University Press.

Burchell, G., Gordon, C. and Miller, P. (eds) (1991) *The Foucault Effect: Studies in Governmentality*, London, Harvester.

Bury, J.B. (1920) *The Idea of Progress*, London, Macmillan.

Carver, T. (1975) *Texts on Method: Karl Marx*, Oxford, Blackwell.

Collier, P. and Horowitz, D. (eds) (1989) *Second Thoughts: Former Radicals Look Back at the Sixties*, Lanham, MD, Madison Books.

Collins, R. (1997) 'A sociological guilt trip: comment on Connell', *American Journal of Sociology*, vol. 102, no. 6, pp. 1511–57.

Connell, B. (1997)'Why is classical theory classical?', *American Journal of Sociology*, vol 102, no. 6, pp. 1558–64.

Copenhaven, B. (1998) 'The occultist tradition and its critics', in Garber and Ayers (1998).

Cottrell, A. (1984) *Social Classes in Marxist Theory*, London, Routledge.

Craib, I. (1990) *Psychoanalysis and Social Theory: The Limits of Sociology*, Amherst, University of Massachusetts Press.

Craib, I. (1992) *Anthony Giddens*, London, Routledge.

Crook, S., Pakulski, J. and Waters, M. (1992) *Postmodernization: Change in Advanced Society*, London, Sage.

Crosby, A. (1997) T*he Measure of Reality*, Cambridge, Cambridge University Press.

Cutler, T., Hindess, B., Hirst, P. and Hussain, A. (1977) *Marx's Capital and Capitalism Today*, 2 vols, London, Routledge.

Dahrendorf, R. (1959) *Class and Class Conflict in Industrial Society*, London, Routledge.

Derrida, J. (1990) 'Force of law: the "mystical foundation of authority"', *Cardozo Law Review*, vol. 11, pp. 921–1045.

Derrida, J. (1994) *The Spectres of Marx*, London, Routledge.

Dicken, P. (1998) *Global Shift: Transforming the World Economy*, 3rd ed., London, Paul Chapman.

Durkheim, E. (1976) *The Elementary Forms of the Religious Life*, London, Allen & Unwin.

Durkheim, E. (1982) *The Rules of Sociological Method*, Basingstoke, Macmillan.

Elliot, G. (1999) 'Via Dolorosa: on the Third Way', *Radical Philosophy*, 94, pp. 2–5.

Featherstone, M. (1995) *Undoing Culture*, London, Sage.

Featherstone, M. (ed.) (1990) G*lobal Culture: Nationalism, Globalization and Modernity*, London, Sage.

Foster, H. (ed.) (1988) *Vision and Visuality*, Seattle, WA, Bay Press.

Foucault, M. (1967) *Madness and Civilisation*, London, Tavistock.

Foucault, M. (1971) *The Order of Things*, London, Tavistock.

Foucault, M. (1972) *The Archaeology of Knowledge*, London, Tavistock.

Foucault, M. (1973) *The Birth of the Clinic*, London, Tavistock.

Foucault, M. (1977) *Discipline and Punish: The Birth of the Prison*, Penguin, Harmondsworth.

Foucault, M. (1979) *The History of Sexuality*, vol. 1, Harmondsworth, Penguin.

Foucault, M. (1988) *The Use of Pleasure*: vol. 2 of *The History of Sexuality*, Harmondsworth, Penguin.

Foucault, M. (1990) *The Care of the Self*: vol. 3 of *The History of Sexuality*, Harmondsworth, Penguin.

Frisby, D. (1985) *Fragments of Modernity*, Cambridge, Polity.

Gane, M. (1988) *On Durkheim's Rules of Sociological Method*, London, Routledge.

Gerth, H. and Mills, C.W. (1948) *From Max Weber*, London, Routledge.

Gibson-Graham, J.K. (1996) *The End of Capitalism (As We Knew It), A Feminist Critique of Political Economy*, Oxford, Blackwell.

Giddens, A. (1984) *The Constitution of Society*, Cambridge, Polity.

Giddens, A. (1985) *The Nation-State and Violence*, Berkeley, CA, University of California Press.

Giddens, A. (1990) *The Consequences of Modernity*, Stanford, CA, Stanford University Press.

Giddens, A. (1991) *Modernity and Self-Identity*, Stanford, CA, Stanford University Press.

Giddens, A. (1994a) 'Brave New World: the new context of politics', in Miliband (1994).

Giddens, A. (1994b) *Beyond Left and Right*, Cambridge, Polity.

Giddens, A. (1998) *The Third Way: the Renewal of Social Democracy*, Cambridge, Polity.

Giddens, A. and Turner, J. (eds) (1987) *Social Theory Today*, Cambridge, Polity Press.

Gill, S. and Law, D. (1988) *Global Political Economy*, Brighton, Wheatsheaf.

Gilroy, P. (1994) T*he Black Atlantic: Modernity and Double Consciousness*, London, Verso.

Goldthorpe, J., Lockwood, D. Bechhofer, F. and Platt, J. (1969) *The Affluent Worker*, 3 vols, Cambridge, Cambridge University Press.

Guillory, J. (1995) 'Canon', in Lentricchia and McLaughlin (1995).

Habermas, J. (1981) 'Modernity versus postmodernity', *New German Critique*, vol. 22, pp. 3–14.

Habermas, J. (1987a) *The Theory of Communicative Action*, vol. 1, Cambridge, Polity.

Habermas, J. (1987b) *The Philosophical Discourse of Modernity*, Cambridge, MA, MIT Press.

Hacking, I. (1983) *Representing and Intervening: Introductory Topics in the Philosophy of Natural Science*, Cambridge, Cambridge University Press.

Hall, S. (1997a) 'The work of representation', in Hall (1997c).

Hall, S. (1997)b 'Culture and power: an interview', *Radical Philosophy*, 86, pp. 24–41.

Hall, S. (ed.) (1988) *The Hard Road to Renewal: Thatcherism and the Crisis of the Left*, London, Verso.

Hall, S. (ed.) (1997c) *Representation: Cultural Representations and Signifying Practices*, London, Sage.

Hall, S. and Gieben, B. (eds) (1992) *Formations of Modernity*, Cambridge, Polity.

Hall, S. and Jacques, M. (eds) (1985) *The Politics of Thatcherism*, London, Lawrence & Wishart.

Hall, S., Held, D. and McGrew, T. (eds) (1992) *Modernity and Its Futures*, Cambridge, Polity.

Halliday, F. (1994) *Rethinking International Relations*, Basingstoke, Macmillan.

Halmos, P. (ed.) (1964) *The Development of Industrial Societies, Sociological Review Monograph*, Keele.

Harding, S. (1984) *The Science Question in Feminism*, Ithaca, NY, Cornell University Press.

Harrison, D. (1988) *The Sociology of Modernisation and Development*, London, Unwin Hyman.

Harvey, D. (1989) *The Condition of Postmodernity*, Oxford, Blackwell.

Hegel, G. (1892) *Lectures in the History of Philosphy*, vol. 1, London, Kegan Paul, Trench & Trubner.

Held, D. (1997) *Models of Democracy*, 2nd ed., Cambridge, Polity.

Held, D., McGrew, A., Goldblatt, D. and Perraton, J. (1999) *Global Transformations: Politics, Economics and Culture*, Cambridge, Polity.

Higgins, A. (1998) 'He stooped to conquer', *Guardian*, 17 January 1998, p. 28.

Hindess, B. (1987) *Politics and Class Analysis*, London, Blackwell.

Hindess, B. and Hirst, P. (1975) *Pre-Capitalist Modes of Production*, London, Routledge.

Hindess, B. and Hirst, P. (1977) *Mode of Production and Social Formation*, Basingstoke, Macmillan.

Hirst, P. (1975) *Durkheim, Bernard and Epistemology*, London, Routledge & Kegan Paul.

Hirst, P. and Thompson, G. (1999) *Globalisation in Question*, 2nd ed., Cambridge, Polity.

Holmwood, J. (1996) *Founding Sociology: Talcott Parsons and the Idea of General Sociology*, London, Longman.

Hoston, G. (1987) *Marxism and the Crisis of Development in Prewar Japan*, Princeton, NJ, Princeton University Press.

Hutton, W. and Giddens, A. (2000) *On the Edge: Living with Global Capitalism*, London, Jonathan Cape.

Jameson, F. (1991) *Postmodernism, or the Cultural Logic of Late Capitalism*, Durham, NC, Duke University Press.

Jameson, F. and Miyoshi, M. (1998) *The Cultures of Globalisation*, Durham, NC, Duke University Press.

Jay, M. (1985) 'Habermas and modernism', in Bernstein (1985).

Jay, M. (1988) 'Scopic regimes of modernity', in Foster (1988).

Jay, M. (1993) *Downcast Eyes: the Denigration of Vision in Twentieth-Century French Thought*, Berkeley, University of California Press.

Jencks, C. (1986) *What is Postmodernism?*, New York, Academy Editions.

Jessop, B. (1990) *State Theory: Putting Capitalist States in their Place*, Cambridge, Polity.

Johnston, L. (1986) *Marxism, Class Analysis and Socialist Pluralism*, London, Allen & Unwin.

Keat, R. and Urry, J. (1975) *Social Theory as Science*, London, Routledge.

Koestler, A. (1951) *The God That Failed*, London, Hamish Hamilton.

Koselleck, R. (1985) *Futures Past: On the Semantics of Historical Time*, Cambridge, MA, MIT Press.

Kuhn, T. (1970) *The Structure of Scientific Revolutions*, Chicago, University of Chicago Press.

Kumar, K. (1995) *From Post-Industrial to Post-Modern Society: New Theories of the Contemporary World*, Oxford, Blackwell.

Laclau, E. and Mouffe, C. (1985) *Hegemony and Socialist Strategy*, London, Verso.

Larrain, J. (1994) 'The postmodern critique of ideology', *The Sociological Review*, vol. 42, no. 2.

Latour, B. (1993) *We Have Never Been Modern*, Cambridge, MA, Harvard University Press.

Lentricchia, F. and McLaughlin, T. (eds) (1995) *Critical Terms for Literary Study*, 2nd ed., Chicago, University of Chicago Press.

Levin, D.M. (ed.) (1993) *Modernity and the Hegemony of Vision*, Berkeley, University of California Press.

Levy, M.J. (1966) *Modernization and the Structure of Societies*, 2 vols, Princeton, NJ, Princeton University Press.

Lockwood, D. (1964) 'Social integration and system integration', reprinted in Lockwood (1992).

Lockwood, D. (1989) *The Blackcoated Worker*, 2nd ed. (first published 1958), London, Unwin Hyman.

Lockwood, D. (1992) *Solidarity and Schism: 'The Problem of Disorder' in Durkheimian and Marxist Sociology*, Oxford, Clarendon Press.

López, J. (1999) 'The discursive exigencies of enunciating the concept of social structure', unpublished PhD thesis, Department of Sociology, University of Essex.

López, J. and Potter, G. (eds) (2001) *After Postmodernism: An Introduction to Critical Realism*, London, Athlone.

Lowe, D. (1982) *History of Bourgeois Perception*, Chicago, University of Chicago Press.

Luhmann, N. (1982) *The Differentiation of Society*, New York, Columbia University Press.

Luhmann, N. (1993) *Risk: A Sociological Theory*, Berlin, De Gruyter.

Luhmann, N. and Habermas, J. (1971) *Theory of Society or Social Technology: What is Achieved by Systems Research?*, Frankfurt, Suhrkamp.

Lukes, S. (1973) *Emile Durkheim: His Life and Work*, New York, Harper Row.

Lyotard, J. F. (1985) *The Post-Modern Condition*, Manchester, Manchester University Press.

Mann, M. (1986) *The Sources of Social Power*, vol. 1, Cambridge, Cambridge University Press.

Mann, M. (1993) *The Sources of Social Power*, vol. 2: *The Rise of Nations and Classes*, Cambridge, Cambridge University Press.

Maravall, J. A. (1986) *Culture of the Baroque: Analysis of a Historical Structure*, Minneapolis, University of Minnesota Press.

Marshall, G. (1997) *Repositioning Class: Social Inequalities in Industrial Societies*, London, Sage.

Marshall, T.H. (1949) 'Citizenship and social class', in Turner and Hamilton (1994).

Marx, K. (1867) *Capital*, vol. 1, London, Lawrence & Wishart.

Marx, K. (1964) *The Economic and Philosophical Manuscripts of 1844*, New York, International Publishers.

Marx, K. (1973) Grundrisse: *Introduction to the Critique of Political Economy*, Harmondsworth, Penguin.

Marx, K. and Engels, F. (1967) *The Communist Manifesto*, Harmondsworth, Penguin.

Marx, K. and Engels, F. (1970) *The German Ideology*, London, Lawrence & Wishart.

Miliband, D. (1994) *Reinventing the Left*, Cambridge, Polity.

Mills, C.W. (1959) *The Sociological Imagination*, New York, Oxford University Press.

Morley, D. and Chen, K.-H. (eds) (1996) *Stuart Hall: Critical Dialogues in Cultural Studies*, London, Routledge.

Morley, J.W. (1971) *Dilemmas of Growth in Prewar Japan*, Princeton, NJ, Princeton University Press.

Mouzelis, N. (1991) *Back to Sociological Theory*, Basingstoke, Macmillan.

Murakami, Y. (1984) '*Ie* society as a pattern of civilisation', *Journal of Japanese Studies*, vol. 10, no. 1, p. 279.

Murphy, C. (1994) *International Organisation and Industrial Change*, Cambridge, Polity.

Nakane, C. (1970) *Japanese Society*, Harmondsworth, Penguin.

Neocleous, M. (1999) 'Radical conservatism or the conservatism of radicals: Giddens, Blair and the politics of reaction', *Radical Philosophy*, 93, pp. 24–34.

Nietzsche, F. (1911) *Ecce Homo*, Edinburgh, T.N. Foulis.

Nisbet, R. (1967) *The Sociological Tradition*, London, Heinemann.

Nixon, S. (1997) *Hard Looks: Masculinity, Spectatorship and Contemporary Consumption*, London, UCL Press.

Ohmae, K. (1990) *The Borderless World*, London, Collins.

Omi, M. and Winant, H. (1994) *Racial Formation in the United States*, New York, Routledge.

Pahl, R. (1989) 'Is the emperor naked? Some comments on the adequacy of sociological theory in urban and regional research', *International Journal of Urban and Regional Research*, vol. 13, pp. 709–20.

Parsons, T. (1937) *The Structure of Social Action*, New York, McGraw Hill.

Parsons, T. (1951) *The Social System*, London, Routledge.

Pearce, F. (1988) 'The struggle for Foucault', *The International Journal of the Sociology of Law*, 16, 2.

Pearce, F. (1989) *The Radical Durkheim*, London, Unwin Hyman.

Pearce, F. and Woodiwiss, A. (2001) 'Reading Foucault as a realist', in López and Potter (2001).

Pettman, R. (1979) *State and Class*, London, Croom Helm.

Poster, M. (ed.) (1989) *Jean Baudrillard: Selected Writings*, Stanford, CA, Stanford Univerity Press.

Potter, G. (1999) *The Bet: Truth in Science, Literature and Everyday Life*, Aldershot, Ashgate.

Poulantzas, N. (1975) *Classes in Contemporary Capitalism*, London, Verso.

Propp, V. (1963) *The Morphology of the Folktale*, Austin, University of Texas Press.

Resnick, S. and Wolfe, R. (1987) *Knowledge and Class: A Marxian Critique of Political Economy*, Chicago, University of Chicago Press.

Rex, J. (1961) *Key Problems in Sociological Theory*, London, Routledge.

Riesman, D. (1950) *The Lonely Crowd*, New Haven, CT, Yale University Press.

Robertson, R. (1990) 'Mapping the global condition: globalization as the central concept', in Featherstone (1990).

Robertson, R. and Turner, B. (eds) (1991) *Talcott Parsons: Theorist of Modernity*, London, Sage.

Rorty, R. (1982) *Consequences of Pragmatism*, Brighton, Harvester Press.

Rose, N. (1999) 'Inventiveness in politics: a review of Giddens's "Third Way"', *Economy and Society*, vol. 28, no. 3, pp. 467–94.

Rosenau, P. (1992) *Post-Modernism and the Social Sciences*, Princeton, NJ, Princeton University Press.

Ruccio, D., Resnick, S. and Wolff, R. (1991) 'Class beyond the nation state', *Capital and Class*, no. 43, pp. 25–41.

Russell, B. (1961) *A History of Western Philosophical Thought*, London, Allen & Unwin.

Said, E. (1979) *Orientalism*, New York, Vintage.

Saunders, P. (1990) *Social Class and Stratification*, London, Routledge.

Saussure, F. de (1974) *Course in General Linguistics*, London, Fontana.

Schiller, H. (1970) *Mass Communications and the American Empire*, New York, Kelley.

Seidman, S. (1996) *Queer Theory/Sociology*, Oxford, Blackwell.

Seidman, S. (ed.) (1994) *The Postmodern Turn*, Cambridge, Cambridge University Press.

Seuren, P. (1998) *Western Linguistics: An Historical Introduction*, Blackwell, Oxford.

Sinclair, I. (1997) *Lights Out for the Territory*, London, Granta Books.

Sklair, L. (1991) *Sociology of the Global System*, Hemel Hempstead, Harvester Wheatsheaf.

Soja, E. (1989) *Postmodern Geographies*, London, Verso.

Tester, K. (ed.) (1994) *The Flâneur*, London, Routledge.

Thompson, E.P. (1964) *The Making of the English Working Class*, London, Gollancz.

Tomlinson, J. (1999) *Globalisation and Culture*, Cambridge, Polity.

Traugott, M. (1978) *Emile Durkheim on Institutional Analysis*, Chicago, University of Chicago Press.

Trigg, R. (1981) *Reality at Risk*, Brighton, Harvester.

Turner, B. (1978) *Marx and the End of Orientalism*, London, Allen & Unwin.

Turner, B. (1986) *Citizenship and Capitalism*, London, Allen & Unwin.

Turner, B. (1994) *Orientalism, Postmodernism and Orientalism*, London, Routledge.

Turner, B. and Hamilton, P. (eds) (1994) *Citizenship: Critical Concepts*, London, Routledge.

Turner, S. (1996) *Social Theory and Sociology: the Classics and Beyond*, Oxford, Blackwell.

Urry, J. (2000) *Sociology Beyond Societies*, London, Routledge.

Vogler, C. (1985) *The Nation State: the Neglected Dimension of Class*, Aldershot, Gower.

Vogler, C. (2000) 'The end of geography: national identities and emotion in the discourse of British manufacturing unions in the 1980s and early 1990s', Mimeo, Department of Sociology, City University, London.

Wagner, P. (1994) *A Sociology of Modernity: Liberty and Discipline*, London, Routledge.

Walby, S. (1990) *Theorizing Patriarchy*, Oxford, Blackwell.

Waters, M. (1995) *Globalization*, London, Routledge.

Weber, M. (1949) *The Methodology of the Social Sciences*, New York, The Free Press.

Weber, M. (1978) *Economy and Society*, 2 vols, Berkeley, University of California Press.

Wernick, A. (1991) *Promotional Culture*, London, Sage.

Willetts, P. (1997) 'Transnational actors and international organisations in global politics', in Baylis and Smith (1997).

Winch, P. (1958) *The Idea of a Social Science*, London, Routledge.

Wittfogel, K. (1957) *Oriental Despotism*, Oxford, Oxford University Press.

Woodiwiss, A. (1990a) *Social Theory after Postmodernism: Rethinking Production, Law and Class*, London, Pluto.

Woodiwiss, A. (1990b) *Rights v. Conspiracy: a Sociological Essay on the History of Labour Law in the United States*, Oxford, Berg.

Woodiwiss, A. (1992) *Law, Labour and Society in Japan*, London, Routledge.

Woodiwiss, A. (1993) *Postmodernity USA: The Crisis of Social Modernism in the Postwar United States*, London, Sage.

Woodiwiss, A. (1996) 'Searching for signs of globalisation', *Sociology*, vol. 30, no. 4, pp. 799–810.

Woodiwiss, A. (1998) *Globalisation, Human Rights and Labour Law in Pacific Asia*, Cambridge, Cambridge University Press.

Woodiwiss, A. (forthcoming) *Making Human Rights Work: a Sociological Approach*.

Yates, F. (1979) *The Occult Philosophy in the Elizabethan Age*, London, Routledge & Kegan Paul.

Index

canon, classical authors as, 22–8
Capital, 32, 36–7, 38
capitalism, 122; globalisation,
    183–4, 190; Marx, 31–2,
    33–4, 36–7, 84; modernity,
    94, 95, 97–8, 100, 101, 105,
    117, 123–4, 127, 164;
    postmodernism, 130
Carver, Terrell, 36, 38
Catlin, Brian, 162
Cézanne, Paul, 144
change: modernity, 102;
    visuality, 159–60
Chicago School, 23
citizenship, 65, 73
class, 39, 64–5, 75–6, 115–16;
    'class reductionism,' 170;
    structure, 168–71; theory,
    127
classical authors: 'canon,' 22–8;
    legacy, 58–61; social
    problems, 158–9
Cogito, 141
'collective representations'
    (Durkheim), 55
Collins, Randall, 24–5, 173
Communist Manifesto, 35, 93
comparative method, sociology,
    53–4
Conceptual Art, 162
conflict theorists, 70–2
Confucianism, 173, 174

Connell, Bob, 22–5, 26, 28, 173
consciousness, social product, 30
Consequences of Modernity, 101–2
Constable, John, 40, 143
Constitution of Society, The, 78, 101
'constructionist' theory of
    language, 89, 90
Cottrell, A., 127
Coxon, Tony, 54
Craib, I., 106
Critical Theory, 69, 107
Cromwell Cox, Oliver, 59
Crook, S., 119
Crosby, A., 140
Cubism, 144
cultural imperialism, 187–8
Cultural Studies, 5, 88, 127
'culture wars,' 26
Cutler, T., 127

Dahrendorf, Ralf, 70
Dali, Salvador, 144
Derrida, Jacques, 14, 123, 126,
    127, 129, 146, 155
Descartes, R., 141
determinism, 113, 115
Dicken, P., 186
Discipline and Punish, 53, 150
discourse, power effects of,
    150–1
discourse analysis, sociological
    method, 54

discursive formations (Foucault), 27, 148–51, 152, 155–7, 158, 159–60; sociology as, 162–5, 170, 173
'disembedding mechanisms,' 104, 106
Disneyland, 138, 145
disorder, problem of, 73–5
Division of Labour in Society, The, 48, 76
Dubois, W.E.B., 59
Durkheim, Emile, 3, 12; globalisation, 181, 188, 194; orientalism, 173; representationalism, 47–56; social facts, 48–9, 51, 52–3; social structure, 55–6

Economic and Philosophical Manuscripts, The, 29, 33
Economy and Society, xii, 41–3, 44
Elementary Forms of Religious Life, The, 55
empiricist representationalism, 30, 31, 33–6, 41–2, 45, 48, 53, 56, 66, 80, 88, 90
Engels, Friedrich, 30, 93
Escher, M.C., 56, 162
ethnocentrism, 124
ethnomethodology, 6, 141
Eurocentricity, 179

European Marxism (1960s), 65, 68–9
evolutionary theory, 79
expert systems, 104

Fanon, Franz, 187
Featherstone, M., 188
feminism, 160; epistemologists, 47; sociologists, 175
'fetishism of commodities' (Marx), 32, 36–7, 39
Formations of Modernity, 108
Foster, Hal, ix, 1, 3, 4
Foucault, Michel: discursive formations, 27, 155–7, 158, 159–60; lessons for methodology, 157–8, 161; semiological project, 153–7; social scientist, 147–53, 157–8
Frankfurt school, 99
French Grammarian tradition, 29
Frisby, David, 99, 106
functionalism, 56, 70–1

Gane, Mike, xii
gender, 23, 24, 59
'genealogical' texts, of Foucault, 150, 155, 156
German Ideology, The, 30, 32, 34–5
Gerth, H., 40, 45

International Non-Governmental
   Organisations (IGOs), 182–3
Intimations of Postmodernity, 119
Islamic Sociology, 174

Jacques, M., 121
James, C.L.R., 187
Jameson, Frederick, 98, 139, 188
Japan: modernity, 111–12, 124;
   unique society, 174
Jay, Martin, ix, 3, 140, 141–3
Jencks, Charles, 145
Jessop, Bob, 189
Johnston, L., 127

Keat, R., 58
Kitaj, R.B., 145, 177
knowledge, progressive nature
   of, 135
Kosselleck, Reinhart, 103
Kuhn, Thomas, 137
Kumar, K., 97

labour rights, 191–4
Lacan, Jacques, 126, 146, 153
Laclau, Ernest, 69, 156
language: arbitrariness, 11–12;
   autonomy, 10–11, 12;
   capitalism, 32; explanation of
   social life, 78; nature of, 2–3,
   5; postmodernism, 128–9,
   139; Romanticist ideas, 30,

40, 47; significatory theory,
   44, 90–2, 128, 140–1,
   153–4; social product, 30–1;
   sociologists' understandings,
   5–10, 12–13; theories,
   88–92; vision-dependent
   representationalist paradigm,
   7–10, 13; *versus* visual
   representation, 178;
   Wittgenstein, 77–8 *see also*
   linguistics; philology
langue and *parole,* 10, 11, 153–4
Le Doeuff, Michèle, 130
Leibniz, G.W., 142
Levin, D.M., ix, 3, 140
Levy, M.J., 96, 102
'linguistic turn,' in philosophy,
   78, 81
linguistics: representationalism,
   7–10, 13, 28–40, 126;
   Structural Linguistics, 9–10,
   10–15
Lockwood, D., 69–77, 83, 167
logical positivists, 6
López, José, 5
Lowe, D., 140
Luhman, N., 104–5, 106, 110,
   116
Lyotard, J.F., 126, 135, 137–8

Mann, Michael, 189, 193
Mannheim, Karl, 158

Index compiled by Linda Hardcastle